C.S. LEWIS: THE MAN WHO CREATED NARNIA

MICHAEL COREN

C. S. LEWIS

THE MAN WHO CREATED NARNIA

IGNATIUS PRESS   SAN FRANCISCO

Cover photograph from the Marion E. Wade Center, Wheaton College, Illinois

Cover design by Riz Boncan Marsella

Published by Ignatius Press, San Francisco, 2006
ISBN 978-1-58617-109-4
ISBN 1-58617-109-7
Library of Congress control number 2005933369
Printed in the United States of America ∞

To Bernadette, Daniel, Lucy, Oliver, and Elizabeth, as always

Contents

Acknowledgments

My heartfelt thanks to all of those people who gave their time and support to this project. The book would not have been possible without your help, and you know who you are. Thank you, and bless you.

Many of the photographs in this book are reproduced with the permission and goodwill of the Marion E. Wade Center at Wheaton College, Illinois. Additional photo credits can be found at the back. Permission to quote Lewis' published words was given by HarperCollins Publishers, his unpublished words, by the Lewis estate, through Curtis Brown. My thanks to all of them.

Beginnings

I am a product of long corridors, empty sunlit rooms, upstairs indoor silences, attics explored in solitude, distant noises of gurgling cisterns and pipes, and the noise of wind under the tiles. Also, of endless books.

—Surprised by Joy

Clive Staples Lewis liked to be known simply as Jack. Plain Jack Lewis, his friends called him, those men who also taught at the renowned British universities of Oxford and Cambridge. Lewis was described by some as looking a little like an ordinary working man or even a forester, with his ruddy complexion and plump face. Yet his words were not those of any forester, for here was the finest writer of children's stories and the most popular author of books about Christianity of his age.

He was usually to be observed in a tweed jacket and carrying a thick, sturdy wooden cane, often in the middle of one of his long walks. He would be smoking a heavy briar pipe, sometimes reading a newspaper or a book as he walked. And if he wasn't reading, he would be talking, perhaps to a close friend such as J. R. R. Tolkien, author of *The Hobbit* and *The Lord of the Rings*, or the fantasy writer Charles Williams. On these walks he would compose stories and invent plots. This was the scene at the end of 1939, on a snowy day with a new, crisp white

Opposite: Lewis in 1938 outside an English country church.

carpet upon the ground of Oxford, making the town strangely silent and giving it an almost supernatural feel. C. S. Lewis was clearly on the move. He had had various images in his mind for many years now, images of wonder and mystery and adventure. He now decided to transform these mental pictures into a book. He had thought of a new imaginary land, new imaginary characters, a new imaginary story. The first was Narnia; the second Lucy, Peter, Edmund, and Susan; the third *The Lion, the Witch and the Wardrobe*. The book was published in 1950, and the world of children's literature would never be the same again. This is the story of the author of that book, Plain Jack Lewis.

🌿   🌿   🌿

Today when we hear of Northern Ireland, it is usually connected with a terrorist's bomb or a soldier's shooting. Ireland has long been troubled, but when Lewis was born in Belfast, Northern Ireland's capital, on November 29, 1898, the second son of Albert and Flora Lewis, times were relatively quiet. His parents were Protestants, members of the community

who formed the majority in Northern Ireland. Albert Lewis was of Welsh stock, a solicitor

These row houses are in the Falls Road section of Belfast, a Roman Catholic stronghold. In past years, this troubled area was often the target of sniper fire.

Lewis as an infant. He smiled a great deal, laughed, and was abundantly happy.

Albert Lewis, father of C. S. Lewis. Referring to both his hero, George MacDonald, and his father, Lewis wrote: "Fatherhood must be at the core of the universe."

Flora Lewis, Lewis' beloved mother, in 1895. Her death changed Lewis' life, and he never quite overcame the loss.

with a deep and dark sense of moodiness, and Lewis' mother, Flora, was a daughter of a clergyman, a loving woman and mother who liked to read long, serious novels by Tolstoy and the Russian romantics. Lewis later described his childhood as a time of "humdrum, prosaic happiness" and was particularly grateful for the friendship he developed with his elder brother, Warren Hamilton, known to all as Warnie. The latter was three years old when Lewis was born and, in adult years, wrote of the birth that he could "remember nothing. . . . It was only by degrees that I became dimly conscious of him as a vociferous disturber of my domestic peace."

Little Lea, Lewis' boyhood home. It was here that Lewis and his brother explored the attic, "that secret dark hole upstairs."

The relationship improved, however, and the two men were to spend large parts of their lives together. As boys, they soon became allies and friends, united in their imaginative games. Those games often centered around Lewis' parents' extraordinary house, with its half-secret attic running underneath the roof, tunnel-like passages, and spacious, bushy garden. But most important of all were the library rooms bulging with enormous and enormously interesting books. Indeed, books filled the house, piled in spare rooms, hallways, anywhere, everywhere. Lewis was allowed to read anything he liked, encouraged in this by his mother, very much the intellectual of the family His favorites were Robert Louis Stevenson's *Treasure Island* and Beatrix Potter's *Squirrel Nutkin*, books that dwelt on description rather than bare adventure and that evoked other worlds and specific feelings rather than presented sheer action.

There were pets too: a Yorkshire Terrier called Tim, a mouse called Tommy, and a canary called Peter. Lewis enjoyed playing games of chase with his dog, running through the house as the tiny creature barked and ran after him. He would talk to all his pets and tell them stories about the animal kingdom that he seemed to make up as he went along.

And there was adventure. Being a major port, Belfast was home to the many huge ships that sailed between North America and Europe. Lewis and his brother would bicycle to the docks and watch these great sea travelers setting out to cross the ocean, filling the boys with daz-zling dreams of the possibilities that could lie ahead so many miles away.

Although Belfast is surrounded by quite lush countryside and by hilly and green fields, the town itself is not very different from most other small cities in Britain. Not as large as London, Manchester, or

The hills of Belfast. Lewis never lost his love for the sights and smells, rain and wind of his childhood home.

Glasgow, Belfast is, and certainly in Lewis' day was, rather constricting and conservative. It is also at its heart industrial, with the grimy docks and noisy, smelly shipyards dominating. Although the city was Lewis' home, he always felt a little imprisoned by the place.

The poor, rainy weather of Belfast also contributed to the shaping of Lewis' childhood. Warnie remembered gazing

> out of our nursery window at the slanting rain and the grey skies, and there, beyond a mile or so of sodden meadow, we would see the dim high line of the Castlereagh Hills—our world's limit, a distant land, strange and unattainable.... And so, in circumstances that

might have been merely dull and depressing, my brother's gifts began to develop; and it may not be fanciful to see, in that childhood staring out to unattainable hills, some first beginnings of a vision and viewpoint that ran through the work of his maturity.

There was also sadness in Lewis' early years. His father had a bad temper and for the slightest of reason would explode into screaming fits. His sons soon realized that there was no threat of violence behind all of this, but they lost respect for their father, and the relationship was

Here Lewis (seated, left) is seen dressed in costume with his brother and some school friends. He was always a romantic and a lover of fantasy. Such thoughts helped him escape some of the pain of his youth.

never a particularly close one. Lewis and his brother were also left alone for long periods of time. But by far the greatest sorrow of all came in 1908. Lewis' mother had been diagnosed as having abdominal cancer early in the year, and although there had been a temporary recovery, she soon began to deteriorate. Lewis remembered "crying both with headache and toothache and distressed because my mother did not come to me. That was because she was ill too. . . . And then my father, in tears, came into my room and began to try to convey to my terrified mind things it had never conceived before." In August, just as dawn was rising above Belfast, Flora Lewis died. Lewis was extremely close to his mother and, as would be expected, her death tore into him. He was not yet ten years old, a vulnerable and sensitive little boy. Yet hardly had his tears dried when he was sent across the Irish Sea to boarding school in England—the strict and forbidding Wynyard House.

Lewis hated it. He described the terrible place as a "concentration camp", disliked and feared the angry, difficult headmaster, the Reverend Robert Capron, and constantly longed to go home to Belfast. There was frequent use of the cane, a strict code of rules and regulations, and very little warmth or sympathy. Although Lewis was not often singled out for punishment, as a particularly sensitive boy, he feared it more than most of his classmates. Later Lewis recalled an incident that took place when another boy lightly balanced a book on top of a schoolroom door. When a teacher entered, the book fell on his head. Unfortunately, as Lewis was the only boy who blushed at the incident, the teacher thought he was the culprit, and poor Lewis was caned.

He missed his family, his home, and the freedom of his life in Northern Ireland. He was isolated and frightened. But one thing happened at the awful school that benefitted Lewis and changed his entire life: he began to embrace Christianity. Lewis' father was a religious man of sorts, and both his mother's and father's families had been practicing Christians, but this was the first time Lewis had read the Bible for himself, said his prayers, and worked out his own religious beliefs.

On the steps of Little Lea, 1905: Front row, left to right, Warnie, Jack, Leonard Lewis (cousin), Eileen Lewis (cousin). Back row: Agnes Lewis (aunt), two maids, Flora (mother), Albert (father).

The religion that Lewis embraced is one of the world's great faiths, originating almost 2,000 years ago in what we now call Israel. As a Christian, Lewis believed that Jesus Christ, a Jewish leader, was the Son of God the Father and was born in human flesh to save all men from sin, to show them the way in which to lead their lives, and to reveal the path to heaven. Heaven is extremely important to Christians and was particularly important to Lewis, who wrote about it throughout his life. He and his fellow Christians believe heaven to be the place where the good, the faithful, go when they die. Hell, on the other hand, is the destination of the bad, the immoral, those who reject God. Some artists and writers have thought of hell as a dark, burning room full of screaming people; Lewis saw it more as a place where the love and warmth of God was never felt. That, for him, was worse than any physical torture.

Although Christianity can be quite complex and difficult, its most essential rules are based on the Ten Commandments of the Old Testament, such as not killing, lying, or stealing, and then on Jesus' teachings that we should love God, love other people as ourselves, and believe in Jesus himself. "Faith comes from the heart as well as the mind", said Lewis. He meant that Christians need not understand the entire Bible to understand belief in God.

Jesus was eventually killed by the Romans because of his ideas, and Christians believe that Jesus died for us, his death a sacrifice to God for all the sins that men have committed over the centuries. This belief—that the Son of God died for all men, including Plain Jack Lewis—was central to Lewis' life. The other aspect of Christian belief—that Jesus came back to life and was seen again by his followers before ascending to heaven—was also crucial to Lewis and was something he wrote about throughout his adult life. Lewis believed that, in effect, Jesus was giving mankind another chance to find the way to God and to heaven.

Lewis' belief in this religion changed his life. Besides saying the organized and structured prayers of the school assembly, Lewis composed his own conversations with God. He prayed by himself, for himself. He discussed religion with the other boys in what he later described as "an entirely healthy and profitable way". Comforting though faith was, Lewis was still desperately unhappy and wrote to his father begging to be removed from the school. Finally liberation came, not because of his or his father's efforts, but because Wynyard simply could not tempt enough students to come through its forbidding gates. It closed down, and Lewis was sent back to Belfast. He was extraordinarily happy.

And he was safe now, comfortable and assured. He read voraciously, science fiction, novels of romance and war, and of course, his beloved Bible. He liked nothing more than hiding himself away in a large hallway cupboard or an unused room with a stack of books and a pile of sandwiches—strawberry jam was a favorite—and with the light of a candle, he would spend hours reading and taking bites of sandwich, reading more and taking more bites of sandwich. On one of these occasions, he fell asleep, and nobody could find him until the middle of the night. When Lewis was finally discovered, he simply picked up his books and walked out of the room as if nothing had happened. He was truly a devoted reader.

In July 1910, Lewis was sent to Campbell College, just a mile from his home. This was a major change from the dampness and darkness of Wynyard. He boarded at the school during the week, but was allowed

Warren, Albert, and Jack Lewis in 1910. A rather posed and stylized photograph of an Edwardian family.

to go home on Sundays. Here he would tell his father of the new delights of the school life, of his English teacher, J. A. McNeill, who read Matthew Arnold's poem "Sohrab and Rustum" and passed on to the eleven-year-old boy the joy of poetry. Lewis was happy and becoming happier. Yet in November 1910, he fell ill with a bad cold, which led to a serious chest condition. His father decided that his son would now attend Cherbourg School in Malvern, a town famous as a health resort.

"Malvern is one of the nicest English towns I have seen yet", wrote Lewis to his father of his first impressions of the place. "The hills are beautiful." Indeed, resting as it does in the middle of England, the town is quite lovely, with its abundant supply of quaint tea shops, country walks, and quiet lanes. There were only seventeen boys and four masters at the school, and Lewis was able to consume the ideas and opinions of his teachers like some new, sweet, thirst-quenching drink. He learned of London and its theaters and society from the teachers' chats, of Virgil and Homer, and most important of all, of northern mythology. The latter left a special mark on the twelve-year-old Lewis, and after he was taken by his father to a concert by the German composer Richard Wagner, with all of its Nordic message and melodies, Lewis was convinced that if God or the gods were anywhere, they were in the tales of the twilight world of northern adventure. As a consequence of this, he began to lose his Christianity. "The impression I got was that religion in general, though utterly false, was a natural growth, a kind of endemic nonsense into which mankind tended to blunder", he wrote later.

Soon Lewis fell victim to yet another illness, a painful infection that sent him to the school hospital, where he also took and passed his entrance exams to Malvern College. It was obvious even then to his examiners, his teachers, and his father that Lewis was an extremely gifted boy. He began at his new school, known to the boys as "The Coll", in 1913. Malvern College was a departure for Lewis, a large school with a great many rules and regulations and a competitiveness he had not experienced before. Lewis had been born with thumbs that did not bend properly, and he found it almost impossible to catch balls or hold a bat or racket in the right way. Hence he was a poor cricket player, and a poor cricket player made for an unhappy boy at Malvern, where sport was given such importance. He disliked most of his fellow students as well, and they returned the feeling.

He was fond, however, of some of his teachers, in particular the Latin master, Harry Wakelyn Smith, known as Smugy. Among the rough-and-tumble boys and the sporty rivalry, Smugy stood out as being gentle, studious, and patient. He taught Lewis more about poetry, how it "should be savoured and mouthed in solitude", and about the poets Milton, Horace, and Yeats. Yeats' writings on Celtic mythology had a particular influence on this young boy already in awe of the northern legends. Then, in the summer of 1914, the fifteen-year-old Lewis was told by his father that he could leave Malvern and be educated privately by a family friend, William Kirkpatrick. If this news was liberating, the headlines in the newspapers and the talk of the school was not. The inevitable had happened, and the great European powers had gone to war. Some thought it would be over by Christmas. Lewis, though still a teenager, thought otherwise.

&. &. &.

While the British armies dug in on the muddy battlefields of northern France and prepared for their confrontation with the soldiers of Germany, Lewis made his way to Surrey for a different kind of meeting. Here he met Mr. Kirkpatrick, a sixty-six-year-old teacher who had taught Lewis' father and who would alter Lewis' life. At their first meeting, Lewis

*W. T. Kirkpatrick, Lewis'
teacher, with his wife in 1920.
Lewis was passionate about
the importance of education
until the day he died.*

explained that he was surprised by the Surrey landscape. The remark was not allowed to pass. Kirkpatrick stopped, turned to Lewis, and began an impromptu lesson. To be surprised, he said, one would first have to have an expectation of the territory, and Lewis had none. The boy's comments were thus meaningless.

This was not an exercise in cruelty, but an attempt to make Lewis think for himself and to challenge his comfortable ideas. There was more. At nine o'clock on Lewis' first Monday morning with Kirkpatrick, the teacher read aloud from Homer's *Iliad* and then passed the book to Lewis and told him to translate from the Greek. Many boys thrown into the deep end of the pool of education would have drowned; Lewis was at first treading water, but then learned to swim quite magnificently. Not only did he learn to translate and love the Greek poets, but also to master French, German, and Italian, so as to read Molière, Goethe, and Dante.

Lewis was in his element; he was being challenged by someone he respected. Kirkpatrick's influence also had its effect on Lewis' religious beliefs. His objections to Christianity were strengthened by his new mentor's aggressive atheism, and he moved further and further away from any church teachings or belief in the Bible. While Mr. Kirkpatrick was directing Lewis' religious and educational life, Mrs. Kirkpatrick was initiating him into the pleasures of London. She took him to the theater there and introduced him to the city's bookshops. Yet none of these influences were as strong or lasting as that of a dead Scottish author whom Lewis came upon quite by chance.

In early March 1916, while browsing through the local railway station bookstall, Lewis picked up a volume entitled *Phantastes* by George MacDonald. He glanced through the first few pages and immediately realized that he had fallen in love with the work and its creator. Lewis would write: "I have never concealed the fact that I regarded him as my master; indeed I fancy I have never written a book in which I did not quote from him.... He seems to know everything and I find my own experience in it constantly."

MacDonald had died in 1905 and had never become a particularly popular author. He primarily wrote adult fantasies involving dreamworlds and religious symbolism, but he was better known for his children's books, among them *The Princess and the Goblin*. He was also a dedicated Christian. There was now a man pulling Lewis in another direction when it came to religion.

Throughout 1915, while the war was bleeding away the life of the youth of Europe, Lewis studied and read. By the end of the following year, aged eighteen, he was ready to sit the scholarship exams for Oxford University. He passed and was accepted at University College. The university and the town were to be home for him for many years, and Lewis never lost his fascination for the architecture and art or the pubs and places of worship of Oxford. His own rooms were comfortable and inviting. Thick rugs, a fire in the corner with tea seemingly always about to be made, a grand piano, and enormous and heavy wooden tables. The poet Percy Bysshe Shelley had been at this college, and on his walks, Lewis thought of the great young man and felt close to him, just as those who came after Lewis would imagine themselves close to the author of the Narnia stories when they passed his old rooms and the places where he had walked.

Oxford is in many ways British history embodied. The town is set in the middle of the Cotswolds, that most English of areas in southern England, to the west of London, where every country lane seems to contain endless possibilities of magic and wonder: a medieval church around one corner, the sight of a Tudor inn around another. Greens and browns do battle to dominate the color of this land, and

Opposite: The war may have seemed a world away to Lewis at Oxford in 1915, but things were becoming more and more difficult for the less privileged in other parts of England. By 1917, as German U-boats cut off Britain's supplies, the government had to impose rationing, and people were forced to line up for food.

rising out of the Cotswolds, almost shining and glistening, is Oxford University.

The Oxford that Lewis saw was splendid in its antiquity, dating back to the twelfth century. Indeed, Worcester College, built in 1714, was considered to be quite modern and new. Wherever one looks are spires, turrets, stained glass windows, and shadows dating back to ancient wars, ancient scholars, ancient ideas. The sounds of the town are of church bells and of old bicycle wheels on cobble streets; the sights are of steaming tea being poured into china cups, of beer filling pint glasses in pubs where Shakespeare might have drunk, and of colleges where kings might have slept hundreds of years earlier. The past was not to be read about in dusty books but to be tasted, felt, and smelled as one walked the streets. This was liberation for Lewis, from limited Belfast to limitless Oxford. It might not have been heaven, but it was a fairly good imitation.

Oxford seemed far away from the battles of France, but this was illusion. As an Irishman, Lewis could not be conscripted into the British Army, but he chose to volunteer. "I'm not a pacifist. If it's got to be it's got to be", he would write. "But the flesh is weak and selfish and I think death would be much better than to live through another war." As he left Oxford for his military training, however, Lewis still believed that glory might await him. He was soon to change his mind.

Dreams and Dreaming Spires

It is a very consoling fact that so many books about real lives—biographies, autobiographies, letters, etc.—give one such an impression of happiness, in spite of the tragedies they all contain. . . . Perhaps the tragedies of real life contain more consolation and fun and gusto than the comedies of literature?

—THE LETTERS OF C. S. LEWIS TO ARTHUR GREEVES

During the early stages of his military training, Lewis met another Irishman, a young man named Edward Francis Courtenay Moore, known to his friends simply as Paddy. The two became close companions, and through this friendship Lewis got to know Paddy's mother, Mrs. Janie Moore. Their relationship would deepen following the end of the war, and Mrs. Moore would become a form of surrogate mother to Lewis. For the present, however, he could concentrate only on what was approaching him in France, and before his

Lewis (left) sitting next to Paddy Moore in 1917. It was a good friendship and a sad parting.

Lewis was committed to fighting in what he believed would be "the war to end all wars", but the horrors of the trenches—like this one at the Somme—soon convinced him that there could be no glory in war.

nineteenth birthday, he was posted to the front line near Arras. He enjoyed certain aspects of this military life: the brotherly feelings of the men and the idea and ideal of the common cause.

Yet as the conflict continued, Lewis began to realize that death was the dominant result of war, and pain and suffering its constant theme.

To his surprise, he took sixty German prisoners almost single-handedly when he "discovered to my great relief that the crowd of field-grey figures who suddenly appeared from nowhere, all had their hands up". In 1917, the military situation worsened, with the bloody stalemate of trench warfare at its worst. Lewis witnessed for himself the dead bodies, the disease, the muddy chaos of this "war to end all wars". And then, in

Crowds gather at Trafalgar Square in London to mark the signing of the Armistice to end the First World War. Even the poor reception given to his first book, Spirits in Bondage, *could not dampen Lewis' enthusiasm for the peace agreement.*

April, a shell landed near the place where Lewis was standing, killing one of his friends and injuring Lewis in the arm, face, and leg. For a few moments, winded and bent double, Lewis thought he had been killed, but then realized that his wounds were not fatal but were bad enough to send him home. For this unlikely and unwilling soldier, the war was over.

On returning home, Lewis was cared for by the Kirkpatricks and by Mrs. Moore, but not by his father. Lewis Senior had been drinking increasingly for some time and was now something of an alcoholic. When, in October, Lewis' wounds required further treatment and he was sent to the hospital, it was Mrs. Moore rather than Albert Lewis who moved nearby to care for him. It was while he was convalescing that Lewis completed a book of poems he had worked on in France. First called "Spirits in Prison", the poems were later accepted and published by Heinemann, with the title *Spirits in Bondage*, under the pseudonym of Clive Hamilton. The book was not particularly well received, but Lewis' disappointment was lessened by the signing of the Armistice—peace—and his discharge from the army and return to Oxford.

The university had been changed by the war to some extent, but Lewis' relish of the place was unaltered. He studied Latin and Greek, but also read Shakespeare and Edward Gibbon for pleasure. He rose at 6:30; lunched on bread, cheese, and beer; and read, read, read. His friend Paddy Moore had not survived the war, and Lewis set up house in Oxford with his friend's mother and her daughter, Maureen. He paid the rent, helped around the house, and acted as a model son. This relationship has never been properly explained, perhaps involving Lewis' feelings because of the loss of his own mother as well as guilt over Paddy's death

Jack, Maureen, and Mrs. Moore on holiday in Cornwall in 1927.

and his own survival. Whatever the pressures on his student life, Lewis did extremely well, graduating from Oxford with first-class honors and a prestigious English essay prize.

Even with such qualifications, teaching posts at the university were scarce, and Lewis was obliged to continue his studies. During the next three years, he was taught Old English and read philosophy and literature. It was hard work, but as he said himself, "The only people who achieve much are those who want knowledge so badly that they seek it while the conditions are still unfavourable. Favourable conditions never come."

A favorable condition for advancement, at least, came in 1925 when a fellowship (or major teaching post) in English at Magdalen College,

Oxford, was announced. Lewis applied for the position, and in May of the same year, the local newspaper in his hometown proudly proclaimed "Honour for Belfast Man". Lewis was actually as overwhelmed as he was honored. Magdalen was five hundred years old, a startlingly beautiful building bordered on one side by a magnificent deer park. Lewis slept in his rooms during the college term, often rising early to make a pot of tea, light his pipe, and watch the dawn rise over the park and see the deer running through the long, damp grass. If ever there were elements of the earthly Narnia, it was here.

As a teacher he was popular with his students, even if he was considered eccentric. He would often begin his lectures while still walking along the corridor toward the classroom and continue as he walked in the door as if nothing out of the ordinary had occurred. He delivered his classes in a firm, crisp accent flavored with a slight Irish twang and containing massive authority. He would end his lectures promptly and regularly at five minutes before the hour, pick up his hat and stick, and leave the

Lewis at Stonehenge in April 1925. The concerned look may be because he had recently applied for a fellowship at Oxford.

The magnificent Magdalen College, Oxford. Lewis was a teacher here for 29 years.

room as nonchalantly as he had entered. Many were the students who wanted to run after him and ask him questions, but few did. He possessed the ability to inspire. The Canadian author and churchman Tom Harpur remembered Lewis as being "extremely surprising. I expected so little of him when he walked in the room, he was so burly looking and solid. He looked a bit like a butcher. But once he began to speak, everything changed. We hung on his words." His reputation began to spread its way through the university. Lewis came to the attention of another recently appointed teacher, the professor of Anglo-Saxon, J. R. R. Tolkien.

This was the man whose interest in Scandinavian folktales and Celtic legends would do so much to influence Lewis' writing. Tolkien established a reading group known as the Kolbitar, the Icelandic word for coal-biters, men who sat close to the fire to talk and read. The group was composed of various other Oxford men who enjoyed reading Old Norse and working in the dead northern languages. Lewis enjoyed the meetings but was never completely at home, remarking of his friend Tolkien, for example, that he could not be influenced. "We listened to his work, but could affect it only by encouragement. He has only two reactions to criticism; either he begins the whole work over again from the beginning or else takes no notice at all."

Lewis was thirty-one in 1929 and described this year as the turning point in his life. He had considered himself a non-Christian for some years, following the brief period during his childhood when he had embraced the religion. Being such a self-effacing and essentially modest man, Lewis did not record the details of his conversion back to Christianity in the manner we should like. Clearly he was influenced by literature and by those around him whom he admired. His friends Arthur Greeves, a childhood companion, and Owen Barfield, a London lawyer, were Christians, and when Lewis went to see these men he always listened to their religious views with admiration and an open and eager mind. Tolkien was also a believer, a Roman Catholic, as were other members of the Kolbitar. Lewis' reading was even more likely to turn him toward Christianity. He had been an avid reader of G. K. Chesterton for some time and that great English essayist, poet, and writer of short stories had brought many to Christianity. In particular, Chesterton's *The*

A tennis party in 1910 Belfast. Arthur Greeves is standing on the left, Lewis on the right.

Everlasting Man, with its analysis and history of religion, made an irresistible case for Christianity.

One summer day in 1929, Lewis was on a double-decker bus in Oxford riding up Headington Hill when he suddenly felt that he was deceiving himself, putting off the inevitable, or as if he were locked in a room. There was only one way of escape and that was to accept God and religion. Shortly afterward, in his comfortable and comforting rooms in Oxford, "I gave in, and admitted that God was God, and knelt and prayed: perhaps, that night, the most dejected and reluctant convert in all England. I did not then see what is now the most shining and obvious thing; the Divine humility which will accept a convert even on such terms. . . . The hardness of God is kinder than the softness of men, and His compulsion is our liberation."

Lewis always had the gift of being able to explain the most complex ideas in straightforward terms. His spiritual journey was intellectually demanding and included many doubts and debates. But while writing

Lewis with his father in 1918. Unfortunately, Albert Lewis died before he and his son were able to mend their battered relationship.

to his brother, Lewis used the story of a student to explain his conversion. The student had thrown a bowl of potatoes at a fellow diner, a young man he did not even know. The culprit had been called before the university authorities and asked to explain his behavior. He could not, and answered, "I couldn't think of anything else to do." Lewis became a Christian because for him there was no other way, no alternative, nothing else to do.

That faith was to help Lewis later that year in a way he had not expected. In September 1929 his father, Albert Lewis, died, at age sixty-six. Though father and son had not been close, the death affected Lewis quite deeply, and he strengthened his friendships as a form of compensation. He became closer to Tolkien, and this and his conversion spurred him on to write. In fact, he was a late developer in this field, with many contemporaries having published several books by their early thirties. Lewis began work on a volume called *The Pilgrim's Regress* in 1932. The book's title is, of course, a word play on John Bunyan's seventeenth-century Christian classic, *The Pilgrim's Progress*. In his first major book, Lewis attempted to explore the contemporary political and philosophical temptations faced by the Christian. He wrote of Marxomanni, referring to Marxism; Mussolimini, describing Italian fascism; and Swastici, representing Hitler's Nazi party and ideas. The book—subtitled *An Allegorical Apology for Christianity, Reason and Romanticism*—was something of a satire and stated Lewis' position as being firmly within the ranks of the Protestant church.

As to which particular church, this was not clear. Lewis always believed people should worship at the closest church that was of the

The Kilns, Headington, Oxford. Lewis lived here for thirty-three years. He also died here. The house is named after the nearby brick kiln.

appropriate denomination and not shop around for a certain type of service or style. He was an Anglican, a member of the Church of England, and though various Roman Catholics and evangelical Protestants have tried to claim Lewis by saying that in time he would have joined their ranks, he steadfastly refused to become involved in doctrinal differences among churches. Lewis had now moved into a house called The Kilns on the outskirts of Oxford, and the local church, Headington Quarry, offered quite a high and ornate service. Lewis attended this, as well as the low and more plain service at his college chapel. What was important to him at the time was his relationship to his God rather than his relationship to a church. There is now a plaque in Lewis' parish church marking where he sat. It is behind a pillar, which would have mostly hidden Lewis from the gaze of others but enabled him to observe everything around him. A fellow parishioner remembers that Lewis always left before the very end of the service and that everybody could hear the sound of his heavy shoes and walking stick on the stone floor of the church. "On one occasion," continued the man, who went on to become warden of the church, "Lewis got to the

The pond by The Kilns. Today a sign warns visitors not to disturb the wildlife, such as the creatures of Narnia.

door of the church and found it locked. He made such a noise trying to get out and the vicar was still finishing the proceedings. Lewis didn't seem to care very much and nobody objected."

The Kilns was to be Lewis' main home for the rest of his life. It is a large, warm house with interesting and inviting corners and rooms. Lewis had a special door built from his room to the garden, pond, and forest just outside, so that he would not awaken anybody when he went on his usual early morning walks. The smells of tea, pipe tobacco, and solid English food, such as potatoes and bacon, mingled in the air; the house's sounds were those of Lewis scribbling away at his lectures, talking to himself as he made changes to his notes and books, and the constant whistling of the tea kettle. Here was Lewis' base, his retreat, and his safety. He lived there with Mrs. Moore, whom he still looked after, and he was joined by his brother, Warnie, who had stayed on in the army and retired on December 1, 1932.

Another regular at the house was a gardener named Fred Paxford. He lived in a small cottage near The Kilns and was heard singing hymns in between chopping wood and pulling out weeds. He was rather a pessimist and was brought to life by Lewis in the character of Puddleglum in *The Silver Chair*. The Kilns was a happy house. It "has a good atmosphere about it", said Lewis. "In the sense that I have never been in a place where one was less likely to get the creeps: a place less sinister. Good life must have been lived here before us. If it is haunted, it is haunted by good spirits."

Here Lewis could work. And work he did. He completed one of his masterpieces, a book called *The Allegory of Love*. He had been at work on this project since the late 1920s, and the book remains a classic even to this day. It is a history of allegorical love literature from early medieval times to the time of Shakespeare, and much of it was taken from Lewis' lectures on the subject at Oxford. Given the intellectual tone of its subject, *The Allegory of Love* is a surprisingly readable book, and it established Lewis as a scholar of international importance. It also brought its author into contact with an editor at the Oxford University Press who was assigned to work on Lewis' manuscript, a man named Charles Williams.

"He is an ugly man with rather a cockney voice", wrote Lewis of Williams. "But no one ever thinks of this for 5 minutes after he has begun speaking. His face becomes almost angelic. Both in public and in private he is of nearly all the men I have met, the one whose address most overflows with love. It is simply irresistible. . . . I'm proud of being among his friends." That the pair should become such good friends was most natural. Williams was a self-educated and extremely well-read man who was an active member of the Church of England. He was also a member, strangely enough, of an occult group known as the Order of the Golden Dawn, which in his case was connected

Charles Williams. Lewis loved the man and was shaken deeply by his death. Yet, afterward, Lewis felt his presence all around him.

with his belief in angels and romantic chivalry rather than the committing of dark acts. He wrote a number of mythical tales, and one of these, a novel entitled *The Place of the Lion*, was given to Lewis to read at the same time as *The Allegory of Love* had been given to Williams for editing purposes. Williams' book dealt with the spirit world, with magic and the power of the gods. Lewis was fascinated by it, and in particular by the lion of the title. Here, of course, was a major influence on Lewis, as can be seen in Narnia's Aslan.

In 1937, Tolkien published *The Hobbit* to wide acclaim. It appeared that Lewis was being left behind by some of his friends in the literary world. He was, however, already working on a science-fiction novel, the first of what eventually became a trilogy. *Out of the Silent Planet* was published in 1938, after first being rejected by two publishers before The Bodley Head realized its potential. The hero of the book, Ransom, is a professor, loosely based on Tolkien, who is kidnapped by two strange scientists, Weston and Devine, who have developed a spacecraft. They take him with them to Mars under the mistaken impression that the Martians are cruel cannibals and will eat Ransom as a sacrifice. In fact, the planet is populated by different peoples, by angels, intellectuals, and traders. The novel is a fast-paced combination of space travel, adventure, crime, aliens, and biblical theology. The reviews were good. Tolkien had the novel read to his book club and reported that "it proved an exciting serial, and was highly approved"; the influential critic Hugh Walpole wrote that it was "a very good book. It is of thrilling interest"; and the early stages of Lewis' reputation as a novelist were established. He and his friends, though, knew that his best work was still to come.

Friends, Gods, and Devils

Friendship is the greatest of worldly goods. Certainly to me it is the chief happiness of life. If I had to give a piece of advice to a young man about a place to live, I think I should say, "sacrifice almost everything to live where you can be near your friends."

I know I am fortunate in that respect.

—The Letters of C. S. Lewis to Arthur Greeves

In 1939, Lewis became involved in an Oxford-based club known as the Inklings. The original society of this name had been established in the university in the early 1930s as a student group, but the name was now taken by a group of academics who met to read and discuss their current work. The name was a pun, having a double meaning: a group of men who dabbled in ink and also had only an incomplete idea of what they were about. The Inklings were to become one of the most productive and intriguing literary groups of modern times.

They met on Thursday evenings, with no formal agenda or minutes or officers, but a common determination to share their writing and thoughts. The group included Lewis and his brother, Warnie; Tolkien; Charles Williams; a lecturer from Reading University named Hugo Dyson; Lewis' doctor, Robert E. Havard; Owen Barfield; an old Irish friend of Lewis' named Nevill Coghill; and any of Lewis' or his brother's acquaintances who were passing through and thought to be suitable. New members had to be approved of by the existing ones, and everybody seemed

Lewis and his brother with their bicycles in Northern Ireland in 1908.

to know the sort of men they were looking for. "Is any pleasure on earth as great as a circle of Christian friends by a fire?" wrote Lewis. "The next best thing to being wise oneself is to live in a circle of those who are."

They usually met in Lewis' rooms, with food such as ham and cheese on the table and always a pot of very strong tea brewed by Warnie. Briar pipes would be almost ceremonially filled with tobacco and lit, and then Lewis would ask if anybody had anything to read. Warnie described one of the Inkling meetings from a few years later:

We had at most meetings a chapter of what I called "the new Hobbit" from Tolkien; this being the book or books ultimately published as "The Lord of the Rings." There was a long argument on the ethics of cannibalism.... Sometimes, but not often, it would happen that no one had anything to read to us, and on these occasions the fun would grow riotous, with Jack at the top of his form and enjoying every minute—"No sound delights me more," he once said, "than male laughter." At the Inklings his talk was an outpouring of wit, nonsense, whimsy, dialectical swordplay, and pungent judgements.

Some of the group also met before lunch at the beginning of the week in an Oxford pub called The Eagle and Child, always known by the regulars as The Bird and Baby. The Inklings were attracted by the landlord, an eccentric character by the name of Charles Blagrove, who delighted his customers with dubious tales of how Oxford used to be and perhaps never was. There was security and comfort for Lewis here among his friends, something he was always searching for. The world might be a troubled, troubling place, but snug with the Inklings, a pint of good English bitter, and some strong tobacco, Lewis could put aside the worries that were just beyond the door.

He also went to the theater and to the cinema. He saw the Walt Disney film *Snow White and the Seven Dwarfs* and thought it very good. In Oxford and in London, he saw both classical and modern stage plays, and although he was always a harsh critic, he was also a generous supporter of what he thought was done well. And he walked, delighting in long and arduous treks around the British countryside, relishing his lunch and tea-time stops at local inns for his food and drink. It was on these walks that many of Lewis' best thoughts came to him, as the cool winds of the rural hills cleared his mind. Such was the case with his next book, part of a group of volumes published under the title Christian Challenge. Lewis' contribution to this series was called *The Problem of Pain*. In

this book he explored the Christian response to pain and suffering. It was a subject close to his heart due to the death of his parents and an essential loneliness that was to be with him for most of his adult years. Lewis always believed that pain could be God's instrument, used to help or teach those

The Eagle and Child, or The Bird and Baby, as Lewis and his friends liked to call it. This Oxford pub is still decorated with pictures of Lewis and the other members of the Inklings.

whom he had created. On the subject some years later, he wrote: "What do people mean when they say 'I am not afraid of God because I know He is good'? Have they never been to a dentist? ... We are not necessarily doubting that God will do the best for us; we are wondering how painful the best will turn out to be."

In 1939, Lewis' fears about the world were realized when another world war threw its evil blanket over soldier and civilian alike. Several of Lewis' friends joined the armed services, but he was left behind in Oxford. He tried to continue his life as if it were business as usual, attending church services at the usual time, taking his meals at the same time, and even meeting with the Inklings, though sometimes there were only two or three people present. As usual, when Lewis was unhappy, he tried to work through his problems by writing and thinking. We can be grateful for this difficult period for, by the end of it, he had written *The Screwtape Letters*, that timeless fictional account of an older devil, Screwtape, advising a younger devil, Wormwood, in the art of seducing men into the dark side and destroying their religious belief. The letters are written entirely from the point of view of the devil, so that God is described as "the Enemy" and people are referred to as mere animals to be deceived and directed.

Lewis worked steadily and quickly on the individual "letters", numbering thirty-one in total, and had them published first in a Church of England newspaper called *The Guardian*. After this, they appeared in book form, in early 1942, and the printing immediately sold out. The publisher reprinted it and then had to print again, and this has been the case ever since. Some of this book's popularity was due to the fact that Lewis had begun to deliver broadcasts on BBC Radio and was winning a loyal and large following. This had come about after he had given speeches to various Royal Air Force camps on Christian and moral issues. He developed a reputation as a good and convincing speaker and was approached by the BBC to repeat his work on the radio. Lewis began his series of lectures in 1941, every Wednesday at 7:45 in the evening.

So popular were these broadcasts that they were published over the period of the next three years in book form as *Broadcast Talks*, *Christian Behaviour*, and *Beyond Personality*. Lewis would sit by his study window and write his talks in laborious longhand, for he had never learned to use a typewriter. He would

Lewis as a young man, staring at the camera as if he did not quite trust it. In fact, he was always somewhat unnerved by technology and never even learned to use a typewriter.

also throw his original manuscripts away, explaining that he never had enough room in his house. (His readers have never stopped thanking him for his writing, but his biographers have never quite forgiven him for not keeping more of his original manuscripts.)

It was *The Screwtape Letters* that stamped Lewis' reputation on the public once and for all. "I have no intention of explaining how the

Headington Quarry Church, where Lewis worshipped. It was on the path leading to the church that Lewis first thought of writing about the evil work of the devil, in what eventually became The Screwtape Letters.

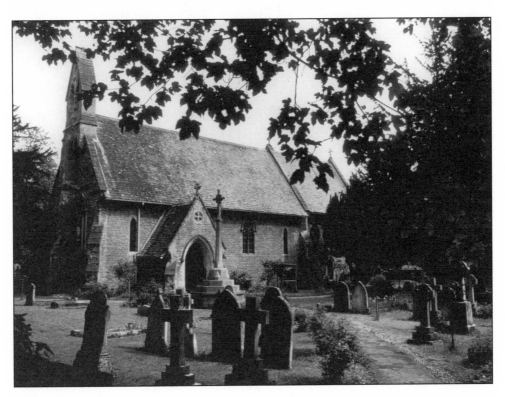

correspondence which I now offer to the public fell into my hands", begins the book. "There are two equal and opposite errors into which our race can fall about the devils. One is to disbelieve in their existence. The other is to believe, and to feel an excessive and unhealthy interest in them. They themselves are equally pleased by both errors and hail a materialist or a magician with the same delight.... Readers are advised to remember that the devil is a liar." One of the most delightful and telling letters in the book has Screwtape advising his pupil to work on relations between a man who is flirting with Christianity and the would-be convert's mother. "Keep in close touch with our colleague Glubose who is in charge of the mother, and build up between you in that house a good settled habit of mutual annoyance; daily pinpricks. The following methods are useful."

Screwtape then describes how the man's prayers should be made to be overly spiritual, concentrating on his mother's soul rather than her rheumatism and thus ignoring the real woman and those things that are of a daily concern to her; he recommends that Wormwood increase his victim's annoyance at his mother's tone of voice, facial expressions, and passing comments. Small things will ensure victory, claims Screwtape. The advice continues throughout the book and is, quite literally, devilish. Wormwood eventually fails in his mission to prevent his man from following God, and Screwtape ends his letters with this terrifying proclamation:

If only we could find out what He is really up to! Alas, alas, that knowledge, in itself so hateful, and mawkish a thing, should yet be necessary for Power! Sometimes I am almost in despair. All that sustains me is the conviction that our Realism, our rejection (in the face of all temptations) of all silly nonsense and claptrap, *must* win in the end. Meanwhile, I have you to settle with. Most truly do I sign myself, Your increasingly and ravenously affectionate uncle, Screwtape.

Lewis was now more popular than he had imagined possible, receiving mail from all corners of the world and in enormous amounts. He was seen by some as a modern prophet, a man with an answer to every question. This disturbed him, although he endeavored to answer every letter that was sent to him in the best possible way he could.

In 1941 he had helped to form the Socratic Club in Oxford with a group of students, remaining its president until 1954. It was a Christian debating society that featured a central contest between a Christian speaker and a doubter or an atheist. The meetings, advertised all over the university with bright green posters, began at 8:15 in the evening and ended at around 10:30. They were extremely popular. Lewis was often used as the main Christian speaker, and he was relentless in his efforts to defeat his opponent. Such was his success that it became difficult to find atheists brave enough to take him on, and debates became tame arguments between rival Christians. Indeed, some who observed these set-piece clashes were surprised, even upset, by Lewis' aggression in debate. He used his intelligence and his intellect, but he also used arguing devices and a cutting wit. He was a muscular Christian, a large and powerful man, and in what he saw as the good fight, he was prepared to hurt feelings. Lewis must not be thought of as a timid, wilting man more concerned

Lewis was a large and powerful man and certainly not a shrinking violet. He once claimed he became a writer because his clumsiness prevented him from making things in any other way.

with the spiritual life and the world to come than with the present. Although he was convinced that this was just a dressing-room where we prepared for the next and greater world, he was also a real, flesh-and-blood character who enjoyed the sensual aspects of his life, whether they be alcohol or substantial meals or tobacco. He had little patience for some of those people who would not or could not agree with him, respecting intelligent disagreement but not empty opposition. If he was a saint, as some people believe, he was a believable, human saint and not an unrealistic caricature without faults.

There were some who said that Lewis was happier when with animals than with men, and although this was not true, there is no doubt that Lewis loved watching the animals that inhabit the English country-side—the squirrels, badgers, foxes, beavers, rabbits, and birds. It was as though they could almost talk, thought Lewis, and wouldn't it be marvelous if someone could bring them to life in literature?

Before Lewis could act on these ideas, however, he had other work to do, other books to write. In 1943 came *Perelandra*, the second volume in his science-fiction trilogy. Ransom is still the main figure, but this book does not have the thrilling story or sheer readability of its elder brother. There are wonderful images: a green lady, floating islands, enormous bubble fruits; and some memorable writing—Lewis described the first thunder as "the laugh, rather than the roar, of heaven"; and a collection of original animals, such as dolphin-like fish who carry people through the sea; but the plot is perhaps not up to Lewis' usual standard. Ransom becomes an almost Christlike figure, giving his very self to whatever might be required so that the world of Perelandra may be saved. He enters the underworld and then rises to life again. This represented Lewis' overwhelming belief in Jesus Christ as his Savior. "The perfect surrender and humiliation were undergone by Christ: perfect because He was God, surrender and humiliation because He was man", wrote Lewis of the man to whom he had dedicated his life. "Now the Christian belief is that if we somehow share the humility and suffering of Christ we shall also share in His conquest of death and find a new life after we have died and in it become perfect, and perfectly happy, creatures."

In practical terms, this meant many things for Lewis. For most of his adult life he gave one tenth of his income to charity; he aided

Lewis' sense of Christian charity took many forms. During the Second World War, when many children like these had to be evacuated out of London because of the threat of bombing, Lewis boarded some at The Kilns.

people in unsung and quiet ways, and when the children of Britain's major cities were moved away from the threat of bombing during the war and into the safer countryside, he of course offered his home for the boarding of these refugees. Mrs. Moore was still living at The Kilns, and she was equally pleased to have some young people, and young help, around the house. A sixteen-year-old Catholic girl named June Flewett came to stay at The Kilns, and though in the end she only spent summer holidays in Oxfordshire, through her we may catch a glimpse of Lewis in the 1940s. This girl, who listed *The Screwtape Letters*, *The Problem of Pain*, and *Out of the Silent Planet* as her favorite books, was unaware as to who lived in this big, messy house and assumed Lewis to be Mrs. Moore's son. June Flewett was deeply impressed at how Lewis prepared Mrs. Moore's bed each evening and catered to her every whim, reading to her until she slept, patient and understanding as this now old lady complained about her condition. Flewett was also moved by how Lewis treated a gardener's assistant who had been sent to the house to help out and to gain experience. He was handicapped, with the mental age of an eight-year-old. He could not read or write but was anxious to learn. Lewis spent hours on end with the man, cutting out pieces of card and drawing pictures and writing letters on them, so as to teach him the alphabet. Lewis seemed on the one hand to be so ordinary and yet, on the other, to be so intelligent and so different from most people.

Lewis was, predictably, unaware of how his house guest regarded him and was anyway too hard at work on his next book, *That Hideous Strength*, to pay any particular attention. This was the conclusion of his three-book science-fiction series, in which Dr. Ransom has settled on earth after his space travels. Retired or not, his adventures have not ended, because there is now a plot to enslave mankind. With the aid of the arisen wizard Merlin, among others, Ransom takes on the powers of evil. Once again there were powerful Christian symbols, and once again the book was enjoyed by readers. "The book is tremendously full of good things", wrote Dorothy L. Sayers, the author of the Lord Peter Wimsey stories, and *The New York Times* said the book contained "brilliant wit, superlatively nonsensical excitement, challenging implications".

But Lewis was not content with such triumphs. In 1944 came *The Abolition of Man*, a concise and striking defence of natural law, a vital pillar in the foundations of Christianity. Natural law says that man ought to act according to the laws of nature, an unchanging set of values common to all men by virtue of their human nature. An example would be that a baby is weak and dependent by nature, thus by nature we ought to defend and help him. An example of natural law being broken would be an obviously strong person walking onto a bus and ordering an obviously old and frail person to give up his seat. Everybody would be outraged, naturally, by nature. More than this, we were created by God and so were our natures, so to live in accordance with our natures is to live in harmony with the will of God. Lewis wrote that at one time, until quite recently, most people believed in an established set of values and assumptions. Now, with Hitler and Stalin in power and the world clearly going wrong, it was essential that we understand and return to the former truths of good and bad, right and wrong. "[The book] is a real triumph", said Owen Barfield, Lewis' friend but also one of his most objective critics. "There may be a piece of contemporary writing in which precision of thought, liveliness of expression and depth of meaning unite with the same felicity, but I have not come across it."

Lewis was most encouraged by this, but was too excited to bathe in any glory. His mind was racing now, and he was eager to devote his energies to a new project, a new idea, a new set of stories, and a whole new world in which to set them. It was time for Narnia.

Narnia

"Who is Aslan?" asked Susan.

"Aslan?" said Mr. Beaver. "Why, don't you know? He's the King.... It is he, not you, that will save Mr. Tumnus."

"Is—is he a man?" asked Lucy.

"Aslan a man!" said Mr. Beaver sternly. "Certainly not. I tell you he is the King of the wood and the son of the great Emperor-beyond-the-Sea. Don't you know who is the King of Beasts? Aslan is a lion—the Lion, the great Lion."

"Ooh," said Susan, "I'd thought he was a man. Is he—quite safe? I shall feel rather nervous about meeting a lion."

"That you will, dearie, and no mistake," said Mrs. Beaver; "if there's anyone who can appear before Aslan without their knees knocking, they're either braver than most or else just silly."

—THE LION, THE WITCH AND THE WARDROBE

Lewis once explained to a friend how certain he felt about heaven, salvation, and the life to come after death. It is just through that door, he said, pointing to the door of an Oxford classroom. It is really no more complicated than that: just through the door, and it is very easy to open it and walk through. God does not want to shut the door; only you can do that. It was this faith in the life to come that helped Lewis through the loss of his good friend Charles Williams. They had spent time with one another both in the Inklings meetings and outside of these gatherings. Williams had been an adviser and a companion, always there when Lewis needed him.

The author and editor was taken ill the day after the Second World War came to a grisly end. He died soon afterward. Lewis was badly shaken and was visibly distressed and upset at Williams' funeral at Saint Cross cemetery. Yet, in a curious way, the death of his friend seemed to strengthen Lewis' belief in God and Christianity. He felt as if Williams were still around him and as if his spirit could almost be touched. He wrote in a letter that "all that talk about 'feeling that he is closer to us than before' isn't just talk. It's just what it does feel like."

In memory of Charles Williams and in honor of the peace that had descended upon the world, Lewis and his friends organized a Victory Inklings, a holiday trip to Fairford in Gloucestershire. Lewis, his brother, and Tolkien stayed at the Bull Inn, where they dined and drank well. They walked through the local lanes, prayed at the local churches, and told each other stories that they were either writing back in Oxford or had just made up. They laughed a great deal and realized that in spite of the recent death of their friend, they had much for which to be grateful.

The return to Oxford was an inevitable anticlimax, with the freedom of the recent holiday seemingly a long time in the past. Lewis had not advanced up the academic ladder in the way that Tolkien had, and he was even quite unpopular in some Oxford teaching circles. This was always to be something of a problem for Lewis. He was adored by many of his students, but did not quite fit in with the established sense of what a professor should be like—he spoke his mind, he possessed religious views, and he did not always say the right things to the right people. In the strictest sense of the word, Lewis simply was not ambitious. So where was his life going? He was a treasured Christian apologist, a magnificent communicator of complex ideas, and a successful novelist. But he still felt that there was more to do, more to achieve. There was, but it would have to wait.

In 1947 Lewis published a book called *Miracles*. This is one of his most serious and complete books, an exploration of whether the universe we can see and feel is the only universe or whether there is a world beyond, a world we cannot see and that is not made of material but still exists, a spirit world in which our existence is only a smaller part of the whole. He took on in literary combat those cynics who complained that if miracles did happen why was it they had never seen one?

You are probably quite right in thinking that you will never see a miracle done. They come on great occasions: they are found at the great ganglions of history—not of political or social history, but of that spiritual history which cannot be fully known by men. If your own life does not happen to be near one of those ganglions, how should you expect to see one? If we were heroic missionaries, apostles, or martyrs, it would be a different matter. But why you or I? Unless you live near a railway, you will not see trains go past your windows. How likely is it that you or I will be present when a peace-treaty is signed, when a great scientific discovery is made, when a dictator commits suicide? That we should see a miracle is even less likely.

The book also threw Lewis into a debate at the Socratic Club, and led him to one of the few defeats he ever experienced. Elizabeth Anscombe was a young philosopher, later to become professor of the subject at Cambridge University. She was a fiery, forceful debater, a woman who could stand her ground with anybody. Later on in her life, when she was being appointed as a full professor, she was advised by the ceremony's organizers that she would have to wear a skirt and not trousers at the installation. She appeared to obey this and wore a long dark skirt, but as she took the oath to accept the appointment, she tore off the skirt to reveal a pair of trousers underneath. Though something of an exhibitionist, she was also a profound thinker and an extremely capable teacher. On top of all this, she was a practicing Roman Catholic, but a Christian who disagreed with much of what Lewis had written about miracles.

The debate took place on February 2, 1948, on a cold and forbidding evening. The room was packed with an enthusiastic audience, each member eager for his own champion to take the contest. Anscombe used her brilliance, her tried and tested arguing techniques, and her understanding of logic and philosophy to push Lewis into a corner and make him appear to be someone who was not familiar with modern ideas. Because Anscombe was also a Christian, Lewis could not use his usual attack that had been so successful with atheists. Each time Lewis made a point, his opponent countered him and thrust back. Lewis parried but was soon on the defensive, and he was not used to it. The audience was shocked. Anscombe was, simply, a superior philosopher and philosophical debater. Lewis lost the contest.

He was dumbfounded. He had not expected this to happen, and he had never before experienced the emotions that follow defeat. He told a friend that his entire argument for the existence of God had been smashed. But this was not the case, nor had Anscombe intended to achieve such a thing—she, of course, also believed in God. Lewis was pushed into despair and was obliged to look again at his beliefs. In this period of darkness, he suddenly realized what had happened. He was living out the humiliation of the cross, and as he had said so often in the past, pride was the enemy of Christianity and being brought low was an aid rather than an obstacle to the following of Jesus Christ. Jesus, after all, though the Son of God, was executed along with two criminals in a horrible and bloody way. His fate could not have been lower. If this could happen to the Messiah, argued Lewis, why should it not happen to his ordinary followers? Lewis came out of this time of anguish a stronger and better man. He also came out of it as a different writer, because Lewis would write no more books of Christian apologetics. *Mere Christianity*, his glittering guidebook to Christian meaning and understanding, was published in 1952, but was in fact a compilation of three earlier works. From now on Lewis would concentrate on children's literature.

Lewis had first considered writing a story for children in 1939, when one of his young evacuees had shown a fascination with a wardrobe at The Kilns and had asked Lewis what was behind it, whether there was another way out through

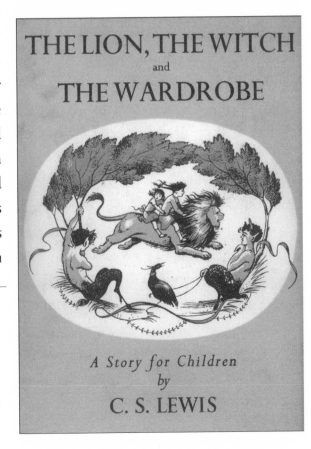

THE LION, THE WITCH
and
THE WARDROBE

*A Story for Children
by*
C. S. LEWIS

Lewis' first children's book was the classic work The Lion, the Witch and the Wardrobe. *Many people thought its publication would ruin his reputation as a serious adult writer.*

the other side. Lewis was intrigued by this and found it impossible to remove the image from his mind. Most of us have imagined at some time or other, perhaps in moments of unhappiness, that all our problems could be solved and our dreams realized if we could leave this world behind. Doors and windows lead quite obviously to another part of our own universe, but what about the wardrobe, dark and warm and secret, the back of it somehow distant but in fact very close. Anything could be in there; everything is possible.

Lewis himself had been fascinated by the idea of the magic wardrobe since he was a boy, when he had read *The Aunt and Anabel* by Edith Nesbit, in which a new and special world is entered through just such a wardrobe. He was also influenced by Frances Hodgson Burnett's *The Secret Garden*. In this book, a once lovely garden is abandoned and sealed up when its owner, a beautiful and kind woman, dies and her husband, Mr. Craven, is overcome by grief. A young girl finds the garden and restores it to its former loveliness. In making the garden live once again, she also reawakens Mr. Craven's love for life and for his son. This is really a story about the resurrection, or the act of rising from the dead.

Another image Lewis had had in his mind since he was a teenager was that of a faun carrying an umbrella and parcels, walking through a snow-covered forest. The wardrobe and the faun, along with "a queen on a sledge" and "a magnificent lion", were the basis for Lewis' first book for children, a book called *The Lion, the Witch and the Wardrobe*.

Lewis always had strong views about children's books, as he did about most things. In one lecture, he said, "I am almost inclined to set it up as a canon that a children's story which is enjoyed only by children

Lewis in 1919, with a beloved book. "Clearly one must read every good book at least once every ten years", he said. And he meant it. One of his favorite children's books was The Secret Garden.

is a bad children's story. The good ones last." He meant that the best stories for young people appeal to their parents as well, and this is certainly the case with *The Lion, the Witch and the Wardrobe*. In everything Lewis wrote, he was trying to make more than one point, and in his children's tales he was also writing of the Christian story, of the salvation of man by God. He used symbolism, representing parts of the Bible—such as the Creation and the Fall of man—with animals and children. Aslan's willingness to die for a boy who has done wrong and his subsequent return to life is clearly based on the story of Jesus. When Edmund gives in to the temptations of the evil queen, Lewis is really telling us about Adam and Eve and how, in the Bible, these first people on Earth picked and ate a fruit from a particular tree even though God had told them not to do so. *The Lion, the Witch and the Wardrobe* is appealing and unforgettable even if we do not observe the religious implications of its story, and Lewis told a friend he would prefer children to enjoy the book for themselves and think about religion when they were older. *The Lion, the Witch and the Wardrobe* is a book about darkness and light, about right triumphing over wrong, about hope and goodness. Like all of the best writing, it succeeds on many different levels.

The book was largely completed by Christmas in 1948, and as soon as he could, Lewis read the manuscript to his friend Tolkien. Lewis had listened attentively to most of Tolkien's work and had usually given his full approval to it, always being enthusiastic and supportive. Understandably, he expected the same sort of reaction from Tolkien, but unfortunately, this was not forthcoming. Tolkien was scathing, saying that the book was not only a failure but was probably beyond saving. There

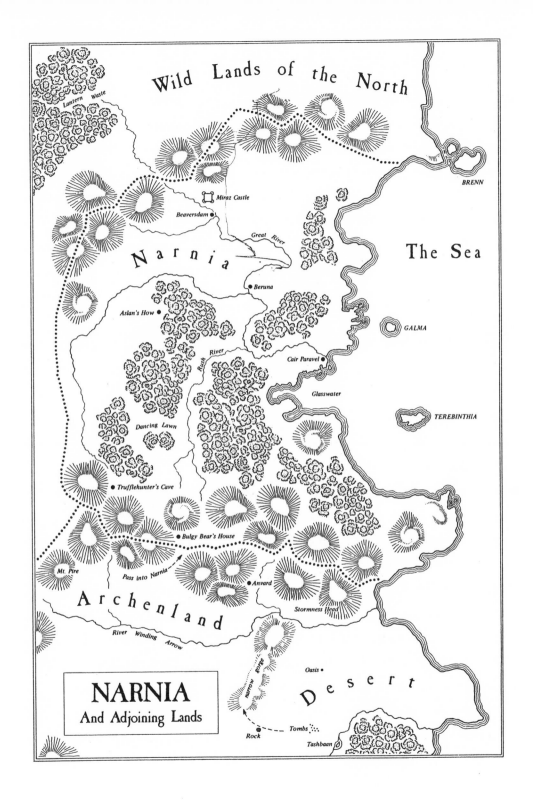

are too many different myths and ideas clashing in one story, argued Tolkien, and Lewis should have known better than to write a book that features Father Christmas, evil queens, talking animals, and children all at the same time. Lewis of course was hurt by these criticisms from a trusted friend, and his confidence and faith in his creation was shaken to the core. It was only the positive words and love for the book from other friends that saved this classic; otherwise, Lewis may well have given in to Tolkien's attack and even thrown the book away. We might never have had *The Lion, the Witch and the Wardrobe.*

Tolkien, however, was not the only person to have problems with the book. Lewis' publisher, Geoffrey Bles, thought a children's book might damage Lewis' reputation. As Lewis wrote to a fan of the book later, "the real children like it, and I am astonished how some *very* young ones seem to understand it. I think it frightens some adults, but very few children."

The book tells of how four children—Peter, Susan, Edmund, and Lucy—stay with an old professor in an isolated country house. "We've fallen on our feet and no mistake", exclaims Peter. "This is going to be perfectly splendid. That old chap will let us do anything we like." During a game, Lucy hides in a wardrobe and finds that it leads to a world called Narnia. This is a land created by a lion called Aslan, where beasts talk and the power of good rules. When an evil witch, the White Witch Jadis, enters, however, the world is divided between darkness and light. For two and a half thousand years these powers fight each other, until the victory of good, the end of Narnia, and the end of the world.

None of this is known by Lucy, of course, when she first tells her brothers and sister about her discovery, nor can she tell them anything of it before Edmund has found Narnia by himself. He is persuaded with Turkish Delight and promises of gifts and power to support the White Witch, in fact the original evil witch Jadis, who had long ago eaten an apple from the tree of life. She is an evil ruler who has cast a spell over Narnia, making it always winter but never Christmas. Because of this, the Narnians can tell that times are changing for the better when they see and meet Father Christmas, who gives the children various gifts to help them in the battle to come. With the help of the good animals of Narnia, the beavers and their friends, the children reach Aslan, the Christlike king. His stature is such that when a beaver announces that "Aslan is on the move", the children react in an extraordinary way, particularly as they have never even seen him. "Edmund felt a sensation of mysterious horror. Peter felt suddenly brave and adventurous. Susan felt as if some delicious smell or some delightful strain of music had just floated by her. And Lucy got the feeling you have when you wake up in the morning and realize that it is the beginning of the holidays or beginning of summer."

Aslan eventually sacrifices his life to atone for Edmund's betrayal of his brother and sisters. But Aslan rises again through the Deeper Magic, a battle is fought between good and evil, and Aslan and his followers are victorious over the witch, evil dwarves, murderous wolves, and wicked secret policemen. The four children are made kings and queens of Narnia and rule their country wisely. At the end of the book and many years later, the four are hunting a magical white stag that grants wishes if caught. While they are on the chase, they find the lamppost that so long ago had marked the entrance to the wardrobe.

C. S. Lewis' Outline of Narnian History
so far as it is known

Narnian years

   1 Creation of Narnia. The Beasts made able to talk. Digory plants the Tree of Protection. The White Witch Jadis enters Narnia but flies into the far North. Frank I becomes King of Narnia.

180 Prince Col, younger son of King Frank V of Narnia, leads certain followers into Archenland (not then inhabited) and becomes first King of that country

204 Certain outlaws from Archenland fly across the Southern desert and set up the new kingdom of Calormen.

300 The empire of Calormen spreads mightily. Calormenes colonize the land of Telmar to the West of Narnia.

302 The Calormenes in Telmar behave very wickedly, and Aslan turns them into dumb beasts. The country lies waste. King Gale of Narnia delivers the Lone Islands from a dragon and is made Emperor by their grateful inhabitants.

407 Olvin of Archenland kills the Giant Pire.

460 Pirates from our world take possession of Telmar.

570 About this time lived Moonwood the Hare.

898 The White Witch Jadis returns into Narnia out of the far North.

900 The long winter begins.

1000 The Pevensies arrive in Narnia. The treachery of Edmund. The sacrifice of Aslan. The White Witch defeated and the Long Winter ended. Peter becomes High King of Narnia.

English years

1888 Digory Kirke born.

1889 Polly Plumber born.

1900 Polly and Digory carried into Narnia by magic Rings.

1927 Peter Pevensie born.

1928 Susan Pevensie born.

1930 Edmund Pevensie born.

1932 Lucy Pevensie born.

1933 Eustace Scrubb and Jill Pole born.

1940 The Pevensies, staying with Digory (now Professor) Kirke, reach Narnia through the Magic Wardrobe.

Narnian years		English years	
1014	King Peter carries out a successful raid on the Northern Giants. Queen Susan and King Edmund visit the Court of Calormen. King Lune of Archenland discovers his long-lost son Prince Cor and defeats a treacherous attack by Prince Rabadash of Calormen.		
1015	The Pevensies hunt the White Stag and vanish out of Narnia.		
1050	Ram the Great succeeds Cor as King of Archenland.		
1502	About this time lived Queen Swanwhite of Narnia.		
1998	The Telmarines invade and conquer Narnia. Caspian I becomes King of Narnia.		
2290	Prince Caspian, son of Caspian IX, born. Caspian IX murdered by his brother Miraz who usurps the throne.		
2303	Prince Caspian escapes from his uncle Miraz. Civil War in Narnia. By the aid of Aslan and of the Pevensies, whom Caspian summons with Queen Susan's Magic Horn, Miraz is defeated and killed. Caspian becomes King Caspian X of Narnia.	1941	The Pevensies again caught into Narnia by the blast of the Magic Horn.
2304	Caspian X defeats the Northern Giants.		
2306–7	Caspian X's great voyage to the end of the World.	1942	Edmund, Lucy, and Eustace reach Narnia again and take part in Caspian's voyage.
2310	Caspian X marries Ramandu's daughter.		
2325	Prince Rilian born.		
2345	The Queen killed by a Serpent. Rilian disappears.		
2356	Eustace and Jill appear in Narnia and rescue Prince Rilian. Death of Caspian X.	1942	Eustace and Jill, from Experiment House, are carried away into Narnia.
2534	Outbreak of outlaws in Lantern Waste. Towers built to guard that region.		
2555	Rebellion of Shift the Ape. King Tirian rescued by Eustace and Jill. Narnia in the hands of the Calormenes. The last battle. End of Narnia. End of the World.	1949	Serious accident on British Railways.

They noticed that they were making their way not through branches but through coats. And next moment they all came tumbling out of a wardrobe door into the empty room, and they were no longer Kings and Queens in their hunting array but just Peter, Susan, Edmund and Lucy in their old clothes. It was the same day and the same hour of the day on which they had all gone into the wardrobe to hide.

They explain everything to the professor, who seems not at all surprised and tells them they should not try to find Narnia again because they will find themselves in Narnia when they are least expecting it. "And that is the very end of the adventure of the wardrobe. But if the Professor was right it was only the beginning of the adventures of Narnia."

This was certainly the case. As soon as *The Lion, the Witch and the Wardrobe* was finished, Lewis began on another in the series, *Prince Caspian*. There were seven books eventually written, and the best reading order is to begin with *The Magician's Nephew*, then on to *The Lion, the Witch and the Wardrobe, The Horse and His Boy, Prince Caspian, The Voyage of the Dawn Treader, The Silver Chair*, and finally, *The Last Battle*. These seven books tell the entire story of Narnia.

The books were written and published at a rate of around one a year for the next six or seven years. It is interesting and perhaps a little strange that Lewis did not write them in the order in which they were supposed to be read, but this was the way Lewis worked—if a story came to him, he would write it down immediately and worry about the order later. It has no effect on the quality of the Narnia stories and only serves to increase our admiration for Lewis the author.

The first book establishes Narnia and its origins, setting the scene for this extraordinary tale and introducing us to the characters involved. The third book, *The Horse and His Boy*, tells of Shasta and his horse, Bree, traveling on an exciting journey from the dangerous land of Calormen to the safety of Narnia, past frightening tombs, dangerous deserts, and terrifying mountains. By the end of the book, young Shasta is forced to

An original illustration by Pauline Baynes from The Horse and His Boy.

The first edition of The Voyage of the Dawn Treader, *published in 1952.*

THE VOYAGE OF THE
DAWN TREADER

A Story for Children
by
C. S. LEWIS

conquer his fear and tells himself, "If you funk this, you'll funk every battle all your life. Now or never."

In *Prince Caspian*, the four children from *The Lion, the Witch and the Wardrobe* are waiting for the railway train to take them back to school when they are magically moved back to Cair Paravel, the castle in Narnia. But the castle and the land are no longer bright and happy, for civil war has ravaged Narnia. Young Prince Caspian intends to put matters right, and with the help of Aslan and the four children, he sets about his crusade.

With *The Voyage of the Dawn Treader*, the Narnia stories take to the sea. While Edmund and Lucy, the younger of the four children, along with their cousin Eustace, are looking at a picture of a mighty ship with a dragon on its prow, the frame begins to disappear, and the three become part of the painting, thrown into the waves. They are rescued by the ship, upon which is Prince Caspian; together they travel to

Fred Paxford, gardener and helper at The Kilns, and the inspiration for Puddleglum in The Silver Chair. *He considered The Kilns' greenhouse to be his private room, and even Lewis had to wait to be invited inside.*

the Eastern Islands in search of the seven trusted friends of Caspian's father.

The Silver Chair features two children named Jill and Eustace and their search in That Place for Rilian, Caspian's son, who has disappeared while on a journey of revenge. They encounter rock-throwing giants, enormous cannibals, and one of the most memorable characters of the Narnia books, Puddleglum, a constantly complaining and worried creature who helps them to safety.

The series ends with *The Last Battle*, which features what the title suggests, a final battle for Narnia. Here Jill and Eustace are joined by Peter, Edmund, and Lucy in their fight alongside the king of Narnia against the enemies of Aslan. The book, and the story of Narnia, ends with "All their life in this world and all their adventures in Narnia had only been the cover and the title page: now at last they were beginning

Chapter One of the Great Story which no one on earth has read: which goes on forever: in which every chapter is better than the one before."

Hard though it is to believe, the reviews of the books were not particularly good, and the sales of the series suffered accordingly. Some people were annoyed at Lewis because they respected him as a writer for adults and believed that he should not be writing children's literature. It is important to remember that, up to this point, Lewis was, and still is, considered to be a writer of books for adults, but as he himself always said, writing is writing and the audience is, to a very large extent, irrelevant. The success of a piece of literature should be gauged not by the age of its readership, but by the impact that particular book has upon its readers.

Word of mouth and the unstoppable appeal of the books soon made up for any poor reviews. George Sayer, a friend of Lewis at Oxford, summed up the attraction of the Narnia stories when he wrote that his stepdaughter began to cry after she had finished reading the tales and said, "I don't want to go on living in this world. I want to live in Narnia with Aslan." In this spirit, many young readers wrote to Lewis begging him to write more Narnia stories. To one of these fans, he replied quite typically: "Thanks for the letter and pictures. I say, you are lucky to have armour: I would have loved it when I was a boy but it never came my way. The kind you have would be even better for Vikings etc. than for Arthurian knights. As for doing more Narnian books than 7, isn't it better to stop when people are still asking for more than to go on till they are tired?"

And Joy Came In

It is quite useless knocking at the door of heaven for earthly comfort; it's not the sort of comfort they supply there.
—LETTERS OF C. S. LEWIS

If God had granted all the silly prayers I've made in my life, where should I be now?
—LETTERS TO MALCOLM: CHIEFLY ON PRAYER

Mrs. Moore, who had lived at The Kilns for so many years, died of influenza in January 1951, saddening Lewis but also freeing him from some increasingly difficult responsibilities. His workload had been enormous recently, with the Narnia books, public and university lectures, letters to answer, and his work on an academic and highly praised book entitled *English History in the Sixteenth Century Excluding Drama*, part of The Oxford History of English Literature series, which Lewis always light-heartedly referred to as OHEL. The book might not be as popular as the Narnia stories, but it added to his reputation as a scholar and is still eagerly read by students of the subject who want a more slanted, enjoyable, and approachable account than most academic books on the theme. Lewis deserved and expected promotion at Oxford, but it soon became obvious that this was not going to happen. One of Lewis' biographers, A. N. Wilson, has explained this by pointing to the snobbery and foolish elitism of Lewis' Oxford rivals. What prevented Lewis rising higher was, according to Wilson, *"Mere Christianity* and *The Screwtape Letters*: the

Magdalene College, Cambridge. "It means rather less work for rather more pay",
Lewis wrote when leaving Oxford for Cambridge.

fact that he wrote them, and the far more damaging fact that millions of people, as they do to this day, wanted to read them." In other words, some academics snobbishly believed that if a piece of writing was popular, it could not be good literature. Lewis did eventually achieve the position he wanted, but he had to go to Magdalene College, Cambridge, to get it. A professorship in medieval and renaissance literature had been created there, and in 1955, Lewis was awarded it. He was happy at Cambridge, preferring the town to Oxford and preferring the attitude of his fellow professors to that of his former colleagues, but he always regretted losing his comfortable Oxford rooms. He had also become very attached to The Kilns and only lived at Cambridge during term time, returning to Oxford as soon as the holidays began. Cambridge was a revelation to Lewis, however.

The other old, great university of England, Cambridge dates from the beginning of the thirteenth century. It is larger than Oxford, more cut off from any city or town, and the colleges—such as Christ's, Trinity, Magdalene, and King's—enjoy green, grassy ground around them and are surrounded by lovely rivers inhabited by swans and small boats rowed by colorfully dressed students. Oxford and Cambridge have often rivaled each other, both as universities and as places of historical importance. King Charles had made his court at Oxford during the civil war, while his main opponent, Oliver Cromwell, had attended classes at Cambridge at the beginning of the seventeenth century. Cromwell's ambition knew no bounds, just as the skies and the fields and the beauty of Cambridge defy all borders. Even today, tea houses, dining rooms, and antique shops bursting with Victoriana nestle between tiny and crowded old bookshops. One can walk through Cambridge at night and be whirled back into another century.

Yet it was not in Cambridge but in Oxford that Lewis began his correspondence with an American woman called Joy Davidman, her married name being Joy Gresham. On January 10, 1950, Lewis received his usual batch of mail, requesting autographs, expressing admiration for his work, and even searching for advice on how to sort out life's problems. Lewis' brother, Warnie, remembered the letter from Joy as being one from just another American fan, but noticed that she soon began to write regularly and that the letters were "amusing and well-written". Most of the

letters no longer exist, but we know of their quality through a letter Joy wrote a friend, the American writer Chad Walsh:

> Just got a letter from Lewis in the mail. I think I told you I'd raised an argument or two on some points? Lord, he knocked my props out from under me unerringly. . . . I haven't a scrap of my case left. And, what's more, I've seldom enjoyed anything more. Being disposed of so neatly by a master of debate, all fair and square—it seems to be one of the great pleasures of life, though I'd never have suspected it in my arrogant youth. I suppose it's unfair tricks of arguments that leave wounds. But after the sort of thing that Lewis does, what I feel is a craftsman's joy at the sight of a superior performance.

Lewis was evidently taking a particular interest in this woman. And that was a little surprising because although Lewis had cared for Mrs. Moore and was fond of the women he had known or knew, such as Dorothy L. Sayers, Sister Penelope, and Rose Macaulay, he had never established any lasting relationships with women as anything other than friends, except perhaps for a brief period when he was a young man. His mother, of course, had died when Lewis was very young, and at Oxford and Cambridge Lewis had known women only as female students. His friends were almost exclusively male, and those few women

Opposite: Lewis with Warnie. Theirs was a successful sibling relationship, and they were as much best friends as brothers. Despite Warnie's initial fear that Lewis' relationship with Joy would come between them, he and Joy quickly became close friends.

he did know tended to be professional colleagues. It was assumed that at the age of fifty-two Lewis would spend the rest of his life as a confirmed bachelor.

This might have been the case if it had not been for the letters of Joy Davidman. This feisty, highly intelligent woman was born in New York City in 1915 and raised by Jewish parents who had abandoned their faith. She was an avid reader as a child and continued this love of ideas and literature at Hunter College and at Columbia University, where she received an M.A. in English. She then began working as a teacher, but devoted most of her spare time to writing poetry. She was a good poet, perhaps even a great one. Her book of verse, *Letter to a Comrade*, won the 1938 Yale Poetry Award. Her novel about Jewish life in rural Ukraine in the years following the turn of the century, entitled *Anya*, was critically acclaimed, and Joy worked for a while as a scriptwriter in Hollywood. She was also an active Communist, and it was within the party that she met William Lindsay Gresham, a divorced atheist with a history of alcoholism and mental problems and a reputation for being a womanizer. In spite of this, Joy and Gresham fell in love, married, and soon had two children, David and Douglas, born within one year of each other.

William Gresham was a talented man, but an unstable one. As a writer, he had some success, but he could not handle even the slightest failure, nor was he suited to a stable marriage or to fatherhood. He neglected his family, and the marriage deteriorated. Difficulties turned into problems, and problems turned into crises. One night William rang Joy and said he was not coming home. He then put the phone down.

Joy was left with two young children and could not even find out where her husband was, let alone whether she would ever see him again. She was desperate and frightened. "All my defenses—the walls of arrogance and cocksureness and self-love behind which I had hid from God—went down momentarily. And God came in", she wrote later of this night. Then she had a supernatural or religious experience. She suddenly felt, or knew, that someone was in the room with her, "a person so real that all my previous life was by comparison mere shadow play". When this feeling left her, she found that she had fallen to her knees, was deep in prayer, and was completely sure that God existed and that he knew about her problems and loved her. Joy was a believer from this point on. Eventually her husband returned, and Joy told him of her experiences. At first he was sympathetic and attended a local Presbyterian church with his wife, but before very long the marriage was in decline again.

Joy began to read Lewis' books. She was captivated, fascinated, inspired. After she had written to him several times and had received as many replies, Joy made the decision to visit England and meet this writer of books and letters who had done so much for her. One of her friends agreed to look after the two boys, and Joy wrote to Lewis asking if he would like to have lunch with her and a female companion. He replied that Joy and her friend should come to eat with him in his rooms. Lewis' friend and biographer George Sayer completed the lunch party, which he described as a great success:

Joy was of medium height, with a good figure, dark hair, and rather sharp features. She was an amusingly abrasive New Yorker, and Jack was delighted by her bluntness and her anti-American views. Everything she saw in England seemed to her far better than what she had left behind. Thus, of the single glass of sherry we had before the meal, she said: "I call this civilized. In the States, they give you so much hard stuff that you start the meal drunk and end with a hangover." She was anti-urban and talked vividly about the inhumanity of the skyscraper and of technology and of life in New York City. . . . After the meal, she asked to be taken around the college. Her enthusiasm, interest, and many impudent questions often made us roar with laughter. I suppose the quantity of good wine that we had drunk contributed to our hilarity.

Jack asked Joy to stay at The Kilns for a holiday with him and his brother. Warnie was proud of the fact that "we treated her just as if she were a man", and drank beer, ate pub lunches, and made jokes with her. Joy did not seem to mind; more than this, she reveled in the attention and the conversation of like-minded people. They met again in December 1952, and Lewis asked her to spend Christmas in Oxford. She readily agreed.

Imagine the scene at the Christmas gathering at The Kilns: the snow falling outside, the comfortable house lit and warmed by a large fire; books and papers covering chairs and tables; Lewis and Warnie and Joy making a huge Christmas dinner; presents being unwrapped and Jack laughing as he opens his, Joy thanking him for hers; tea, hot chocolate, beer, turkey sandwiches in the evening, as they discuss the nature of Christmas, Jack saying, "I feel exactly as you do about the horrid

Joy in profile. She was Lewis' "miracle", and their relationship was one of the great literary romances of the age.

commercial racket they have made out of Christmas", and then talking about the ultimate magic, that of a tiny baby born crying and defenceless and then becoming the king of the world. Joy hung on every word. Lewis sang some songs, he and Joy read from their works in progress and commented on each other's writing. They walked outside. There was not very much lighting outside The Kilns; it was very dark, and they could clearly see the stars and the shapes they made in the sky. It was a very special day and a very special night.

A little before Joy left she received a letter from her husband in the United States. He explained in cold and clinical tones that he was in love with another woman and wanted a divorce from Joy. It was an extraordinary letter, telling Joy that this new woman was right for him because she was only interested in "taking care of her husband and children and making a home for them", and dismissing Joy from his life except as the mother of his children. If Joy had been in America, she probably would have written to Lewis; as it was, she was sitting next to him in Oxford, so why not ask for his advice there and then? She did, and he advised her to grant the divorce, leave her husband, and take the children with her. Joy rejected the advice on Christian grounds and decided to try at the marriage once more with her husband in the United States. But he was drinking again, was still having an affair with the woman he told Joy about, and it would likely have been hopeless, foolish, and perhaps even dangerous for Joy to have stayed with him. The divorce proceeded, and Joy, short of money and sure that England would be a cheaper place to live, set sail with her two sons.

She sent the boys to Dane Court, an expensive school in Surrey, and was almost certainly helped financially by Lewis in this. Joy did some journalistic work and managed to earn some money, but matters were far from settled or secure for her. In December 1953, Joy took the boys to Oxford to visit Lewis at The Kilns. The visit was a great success. "Last week we entertained a lady from New York with her boys", Lewis wrote to another correspondent from the United States. "Can you imagine two crusted old bachelors in such a situation? It however went swimmingly, though it was very, very exhausting; the energy of the American small boy is astonishing. This pair thought nothing of a four

mile hike across broken country as an incident in a day of ceaseless activity, and when we took them up Magdalen tower, they said as soon as they got back to the ground, 'Let's do it again!'"

Joy was concerned about how Lewis would relate to her sons; she was less

The famous tower at Magdalen College. This was just one of the many sights Lewis showed to Joy's two sons, Douglas and David, during their first visit to Oxford.

worried about how David and Douglas would get on with Lewis, because they were already Narnia fans. She had no cause to be nervous about Lewis' attitude, however. "Both boys were a big success with the Lewises", she wrote. "Jack reverted completely to schoolboy tactics and went charging ahead with the boys through all the thorniest, muddiest, steepest places; Warnie and I meanwhile trailing behind and feeling very old." The Lewis brothers taught David chess, and Douglas was shown how to chop wood for the fire. "Without being in the least priggish they struck us as being amazingly adult by their standards and one could talk to them as one would to grown-ups—though the next moment they would be wrestling like puppies on the sitting-room floor", wrote Lewis.

Eight-year-old Douglas had a different experience. As an adult he remembered that at first he had been disappointed. "You read books about princes fighting dragons, you rather expect the man who wrote them to wear armour—at least—and carry a sword, and Jack didn't. He was rather stooped, and balding with a lined, humorous face; he looked like a benevolent and kindly old man, but it didn't fit with the image of a man who wrote great heroic sagas. But the disappointment only lasted about five minutes." Douglas noticed a heavy old wardrobe standing in the hallway of the house. He was breathless. Could this be it, was it *the* wardrobe, was it the entrance to Narnia? Lewis smiled and said mysteriously that it might just be. Douglas refused to hang his coat in it for years.

Nine-year-old David also enjoyed the visit and indeed remained extremely fond of Lewis. Later in his life, David embraced the Judaism that his mother had abandoned for Christianity. It is an interesting insight into Lewis' tolerance toward Judaism that he never tried to convert David to Christianity and, in fact, wrote to various Jewish friends of his asking for advice on how to make it easier for David to practice his faith, how to give him a Kosher diet, and so on. It is true to say that at no time in his life did Lewis show any signs of religious bigotry.

The visit ended. Lewis continued with his writing, Joy got on with sending the children to school and working on her own poetry and journalism. She completed a book, *Smoke on the Mountain*, which included a foreword from Lewis. It did well, but not well enough to clear Joy of debt and financial difficulty. Lewis again helped out. It was clear that the

The wardrobe through which Lewis stepped into immortality.

two people had developed a great affection for each other. There was no alternative, said Lewis, and Joy would have to come to Oxford if she was to survive with two small boys and so little money and support. In the summer of 1955, she moved to a house only a mile away from The Kilns, and Lewis insisted on paying the rent. Joy and Lewis began to see each other every day, and it was obvious to their friends, and particularly to Warnie, that the relationship was now extremely deep and serious. By this time, Joy was divorced from her husband, and he had already remarried. All seemed well for Joy until 1956, when the British Home Office refused to renew the visitor's visa for her and her children. This meant she would have to return to the United States, unless she could obtain British citizenship. One of the few ways of becoming a British citizen is to marry a British citizen. Lewis was, of course, a British citizen.

Some have suggested that Joy was always intent on marrying Lewis, but this is probably untrue. She wanted desperately to remain in Britain, and she could think of no other way of achieving this than by marrying someone who had, anyway, become her best friend. Lewis agreed, defending himself by arguing that it would be only a civil marriage and be of concern to the legal authorities and to nobody else. Yet what was the status of all this in the eyes of God? Marriage was for life: this was something Lewis had written and broadcast about in the past. Some of Lewis' friends advised him not to go ahead, but Lewis repeated his earlier statements, stressing that there would be no church wedding and that a civil marriage would make no difference to his relationship with Joy. This was probably a little naive, and certainly there are still arguments among Lewis' supporters and those who knew him about what was occurring at this time. Some argue that Joy was pressuring Lewis to marry her in a romantic as well as a legal manner and for the two of them to live together; others say that they were falling deeper in love all the time and that something more than a mere legal marriage was inevitable. Either way, Joy and Lewis were married on April 23—Saint George's Day and Shakespeare's birthday—1956, at the Oxford Registry Office.

Soon the state of this marriage was tested again. The lease at Joy's house came to an end, and she was told she would have to move. But to where? There was one obvious choice. "All arrangements had been made for the installation of the family at The Kilns, when disaster overtook us", wrote Warnie. Joy was in her kitchen with a tray of tea things when she fell violently to the floor. She felt a bone in her left leg snap, and she was in terrible pain. When she was taken to hospital, she told the doctors that her leg had hurt for some time, but that she had put this down to rheumatism. No, the doctors said, it was not rheumatism; it was cancer.

Joy had cancer in other parts of her body as well, and the doctors held out little hope. Here she was, in agony and at her least attractive and physically appealing, and at this moment, Plain Jack Lewis realized how profoundly in love he was with Joy Davidman. Lewis stated: "Years ago, when I wrote about medieval love-poetry and described its strange, half-make-believe, 'religion of love', I was blind enough to treat this as an almost purely literary phenomenon. I know better now." Joy's cancer was diagnosed, and Lewis' love for her realized just after the final Narnia story had been published. How intriguing that Lewis had written in that conclusion to his tales of wonder that "they found themselves facing great golden gates. And for a moment none of them was bold enough to try if the gates would open.... 'Dare we? Is it right? Can it be meant for *us*?' But while they were standing thus a great horn, wonderfully loud and sweet, blew from somewhere inside that walled garden and the gates swung open."

Joy was taken into the Churchill Hospital to begin her ordeal of operations and treatment, and her sons went to live at The Kilns. Lewis now decided that he wanted to marry Joy in a Christian ceremony, before God and before the world at large. No secrecy this time, but celebration and observance. Lewis asked the bishop of Oxford for permission for the marriage to take place within the Church of England, but the bishop refused. Lewis argued that William Gresham had already been married once when he married Joy, and since Christianity regarded marriage as being for life, William's marriage to Joy was not valid. Hence she had not been married until she married Lewis. The argument was clever, but perhaps questionable. The Church's position remained that remarriage by a divorced person whose spouse is living is an act of adultery and that it cannot sanction such a thing.

Those who knew Joy at this time found her to be quite irresistible. Warnie had been suspicious of the relationship at first, reluctant to lose the companionship of his brother. This did not happen, of course, and Warnie soon became one of Joy's greatest admirers. He wrote in his diary that "since she was struck down ... her pluck and her cheerfulness are beyond praise, and she talks of her disease and its fluctuations as if she were describing the experiences of a friend of hers."

But things were getting worse rather than better. For Lewis, the whole experience was difficult to accept, almost impossible to understand. At long last he had found love, only to have it snatched from him at the greatest moment of happiness. He tried to rationalize his and Joy's suffering, and in one of his most optimistic moments, wrote, "I feel now that I can bear, not too unhappily, whatever is to come." But he was too optimistic, and the long dark nights alone were a different matter. He prayed and he hoped and he dreamed.

One moment of relief came when one of Lewis' former students who had since become an Anglican priest, Peter Bide, visited The Kilns. Many who knew him believed that Bide had been blessed with the gift of Christian healing, and he offered to lay hands on Joy. If he was going to do this, said Lewis, why not marry the two of them at the same time? This was an unfair request, because Bide was only a priest and a bishop had already refused to conduct this ceremony, but Lewis was determined to ease Joy's remaining moments on earth.

On Thursday, March 21, 1957, at eleven o'clock in the morning, Joy and Lewis were married in a ward of Wingfield Hospital, with Joy propped up on a stack of white pillows, and Warnie and a nurse looking on. Rings and vows were exchanged, and Joy smiled through her pain. Father Bide placed his hands on Joy's head and prayed for her recovery. Everyone in the room closed his eyes, but nobody prayed as hard as Lewis. Indeed, Jack Lewis had never prayed so hard before in his life.

Joy begged her doctors to let her return to The Kilns. If she was to die, she said, then let her die in the house of her husband. A week later she was allowed to leave, and Lewis and Warnie set up a bedroom for her in the downstairs sitting-room. Lewis became Joy's nurse, looking after her day and night. Fifty-nine years old, he was not a young man now, and the strain and the pain were beginning to take their toll. Warnie was a moral, but not always a physical, help, because he was now drinking a lot and was often incapable of lifting a finger. Added to all of this were David and Douglas, aware that their mother was terribly ill. Lewis knew what they were feeling because he had experienced the same fears and loneliness so many years earlier when his own mother had died. A bond developed between Lewis and the boys, and when William Gresham callously wrote to Lewis and Joy demanding that his sons return to him when Joy died, Lewis wrote back thus: "Your letter reached Joy after a day of agony. The effect was devastating. She felt that the only earthly hope she now has has been taken away." He concluded, "You have a chance to soothe, instead of aggravating, the miseries of a woman you once loved. You have a chance of recovering at some future date, instead of alienating forever, the love and respect of your children. For God's sake take it and yield to the deep wishes of everyone concerned except yourself." William Gresham was persuaded by the letter. If he hadn't have been, Lewis would have fought to keep the boys.

Shortly after this, an astounding thing happened. As Joy felt some relief from the pain in her legs, Lewis began to experience great pain in his. He had prayed so hard for her, certainly asked God to ease her suffering and give it to him instead. Was this a miracle, was it a blessing, or was it a mere coincidence? Lewis was too sophisticated and humble to give a definite answer. All the doctors were prepared to say

Lewis with David and Douglas Gresham at The Kilns in 1957.

was that the progress of the cancer had stopped, which was in itself highly unusual. Yet they still held out no long-term hope for Joy. Time went by, and Joy's bones grew stronger, her health improved, and Lewis wondered whether he dare be optimistic. "Forbidden and torturing hopes will intrude on us both", he wrote. "In short, a dungeon is never harder to bear than when the door is open and the sunshine and bird song float in."

As 1957 went on, Joy was still improving. She was sitting up, then climbing stairs and walking in the garden. A miracle? Joy seemed to think so. She and Lewis fell more deeply in love, and Douglas thought there had not been any two people in history more devoted to one another. "I am experiencing what I thought would never be mine", said

Lewis. "I never thought I would have in my sixties the happiness that passed me by in my twenties." He could now let Joy look after herself, and he returned to his writing. Joy was his best and most accomplished critic. She helped him with a book called *Reflections on the Psalms* and was never afraid to tell her husband exactly what she thought of his work, often in very straightforward terms. Joy was not a wilting flower. Warnie recorded in his diary an incident early on in their friendship when, in the middle of a lunch at Magdalen College, Oxford, Joy exclaimed, "Is there anywhere in this monastic establishment where a lady can relieve herself?" The men with her were as impressed as they were surprised.

Joy also took over the organization and finances of the house. Lewis was notoriously and delightfully forgetful when it came to money, often unaware that he was owed large sums of money from publishers or that his bank account was full rather than empty. Joy made sure that lunches as well as finances were balanced, helped file Lewis' papers, and always, always debated his ideas with him, refusing to let him get away with unformed opinions or unqualified statements. She also tidied up. Lewis'

home had been known by some friends as "The Midden", an old Norse word meaning a dunghill or refuse heap. Lewis had not minded

Joy in front of The Kilns—some might say "on guard" in front of The Kilns, because she once frightened away trespassers with a shotgun.

Lewis, on the right, with his father, brother, and some friends sitting in the sand. Holidays, Lewis always said, were special times to be spent with special people. Two of the most meaningful trips he ever took were with Joy soon after they were married.

torn carpets or falling down curtains, indeed in his rooms at Oxford he had insisted that when friends dropped ash onto the rug from their pipes or cigarettes, they rub it in with their shoes rather than clean it up. The Kilns was more pleasing than it had ever been in the past.

Some of Lewis' friends resented what they saw as the intrusion of a woman into the great man's life. He had less opportunity to talk the night away in the pub or walk for hours with his university chums. But the point they missed was that this was what Lewis wanted and that he had never been as happy before. Joy certainly didn't stop Lewis from seeing his friends, and those who thought this was the case simply didn't understand Lewis or Joy.

In July 1958, Lewis took his wife first to Wales and then to Ireland for a late honeymoon. They flew for the first time and, though terrified, loved the experience of it. They walked the hills and valleys, talked and laughed, relished every moment. Could life be any better than this, Lewis wondered.

Perhaps it couldn't, but certainly it could get worse. In October 1959, Joy went to the hospital for a routine check-up and x-ray. The cancer had returned.

The disease was spreading rapidly now, throughout Joy's body. More prayer, more tears, more pain. Lewis was determined not to let the horror interfere with Joy's happiness. They would go to Greece for a holiday in spite of Joy's worsening condition. Plans were made for the vacation, but would they be carried out? Joy was now riddled with cancer and was in constant pain. The doctors advised them not to go abroad, but Joy was determined. "I'd rather go out with a bang than a whimper, particularly on the steps of the Parthenon!" she said. At the beginning of April 1960, they set off. Joy did better than anyone had expected, visiting Mycenae and Athens, carving out a holiday between her sessions in bed and her inability to walk at all. "Joy knew she was dying. I knew she was dying, and *she* knew I knew she was dying", said Lewis. "But when we heard the shepherds playing their flutes in the hills it seemed to make no difference."

Once back in Oxford, there were no flutes to be heard, and the nearness of death became reality once again. More operations ensued; more time in the hospital, followed by recuperation at The Kilns. It was worse all the time, a gradual failing of Joy's limbs and organs. On July 12, Joy looked a little better; she and Lewis had a long, quiet conversation. "If you can—if it is allowed—come to me when I too am on my death bed", said Lewis. "Allowed!" replied Joy. "Heaven would have a job to hold me; and as for Hell, I'd break it into bits."

The next morning Warnie heard terrible screams and found Joy on the floor in agony. She was rushed to the hospital, where the doctors tried to ease her suffering. It was only a matter of hours now. The day went on, and on. She was given absolution. Finally, as early evening gave way to night, Joy Lewis gave way to death. Before she died, she turned to her husband and said simply, "You have made me happy." And then, "I am at peace with God." At 10:15 P.M. she was gone.

Clive Staples Lewis, Plain Jack, was in his early sixties and a widower. He was also perhaps the unhappiest man on earth.

Out of the Shadows

Grief still feels like fear. Perhaps, more strictly, like suspense. Or like waiting; just hanging about waiting for something to happen. It gives life a permanently provisional feeling. It doesn't seem worth starting anything. I can't settle down. I yawn, I fidget, I smoke too much. Up till this I always had too little time. Now there is nothing but time.

Almost pure time, empty successiveness.

—A GRIEF OBSERVED

This was the first time Lewis had seen a natural death. He had seen men die in war, bloody and bruised, but never seen someone decay into death. He was in a state of shock and traveled home from the hospital numb and disbelieving. He arrived at The Kilns and told his brother. "God rest her soul", wrote Warnie. "I miss her to a degree which I would not have imagined possible." Douglas had been called back from his school. He walked in through the door and saw Lewis. "Oh, Jack!" he said and then began to weep. Lewis rushed over to him and put his arms around the young man. They stood in the middle of the room hugging each other.

Monday, July 18, was Joy's funeral. The service at Headington Crematorium was quiet and rather flat, with few of Lewis' friends present. Lewis was physically and emotionally exhausted, and when Joy's name was mentioned, he would cry. Some people were surprised by this, expecting him to be some godlike figure who was immune to such commonplace grief. If they had known Lewis better, they would have realized

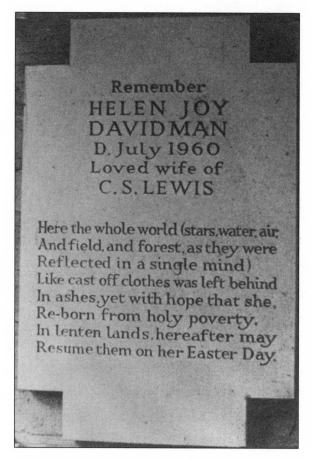

Remember
HELEN JOY
DAVIDMAN
D. July 1960
Loved wife of
C. S. LEWIS

Here the whole world (stars, water, air,
And field, and forest, as they were
Reflected in a single mind)
Like cast off clothes was left behind
In ashes, yet with hope that she,
Re-born from holy poverty,
In lenten lands, hereafter may
Resume them on her Easter Day.

Joy's grave. "You may well know", wrote Lewis to a friend, "that I may soon be, in rapid succession, a bridegroom and a widower. There may, in fact, be a deathbed marriage."

that he never claimed such a position—he was an ordinary man who just happened to be blessed with a genius for writing and communication. "My heart and body are crying out, come back, come back.... But I know this is impossible. I know that the thing I want is exactly the thing I can never get. The old life, the jokes, the drinks, the arguments, the lovemaking ..."

Nor was Lewis' religion easing his pain. He still believed in what he had always believed, but he had never been tested like this before. What hurt him most was that he could no longer remember Joy's face very clearly and did not even have a good photograph of her to remind him. He was angry and frustrated: Why could he not recall her, why were his prayers not helping him, why was the door firmly locked? He applied his severely logical mind to the problem and raised a terrifying question: God existed, he knew that, but what if God were bad, and men were mere rats in a laboratory experiment with God a supreme scientist?

In typical Lewis manner, he decided to write his doubts and worries away. He filled three exercise books with notes about his thoughts, debating his concerns and his grief over and over again. Slowly he saw through his pain. "I have gradually been coming to feel that the door is no longer shut and bolted. Was it my own frantic need that slammed it in my face? The time when there is nothing at all in your soul except a cry for help may be just the time when God can't give it: you are like a drowning man who can't be helped because he clutches and grabs. Perhaps your own reiterated cries deafen you to the voice you hoped to hear." In other words, Lewis was fighting and resisting instead of just being still and asking God to help him, as Joy had done when William Gresham left her alone and in pain. Lewis soon discovered that the less he mourned Joy, the closer he felt to her, as if his despair had blocked her out. Then, when he least expected it, he could remember her face, as vividly and closely as if she were standing next to him, laughing as she talked about literature or beer or God. Joy had returned.

Lewis wrote about his experiences following the death of his wife in one of the most remarkable books of all time on the subject, a relatively brief work entitled *A Grief Observed*, which was not published under Lewis' name until after his death and in which he referred to Joy as H. It is as though he had recorded his feelings of profound sorrow and loss on a cassette recorder and was now playing back the tape for the benefit of anyone who would listen. Such clarity of thought during such a horrible time is rare enough in itself, but added to this is Lewis' overwhelming wisdom. On the way he felt after Joy's death, for example, he wrote:

At other times it feels like being mildly drunk, or concussed. There is a sort of invisible blanket between the world and me. I find it hard to take in what anyone says. Or perhaps, hard to want to take it in. It is so uninteresting. Yet I want the others to be about me. I dread the moments when the house is empty. If only they would talk to one another and not to me.

There are moments, most unexpectedly, when something inside me tries to assure me that I don't really mind so much, not so very much, after all. Love is not the whole of a man's life. I was happy before I ever met H. I've plenty of what are called "resources". People get over these things. Come, I shan't do so badly. One is ashamed to listen to this voice but it seems for a little to be making out a good case. Then comes a sudden jab of red-hot memory and all this "commonsense" vanishes like an ant in the mouth of a furnace.

How accurate Lewis is, and how well he describes those feelings many of us have felt. He goes on to discuss his experience and describe how he came to terms with the death of his wife and to carve out a life for himself without the one woman he had come to love so deeply. It is a work of great courage and inestimable emotion.

During the previous few years, the happy times with Joy, Lewis had also been writing. He had completed and published his only volume of auto-biography, entitled *Surprised by Joy*. The book tells us about Lewis' early life, about his academic progress, and about his Christian life. Strangely enough, the book was written before Lewis had gotten to know Joy very well, and the title did not refer to her. The other important book of the period was *The Four Loves*, originally a series of radio broadcasts by Lewis on the quartet of different loves that he believed we can experience. Lewis complained that contemporary society believed only erotic love existed, but he argued that there were other forms of love that we should be aware of and attempt to understand. The book contains Lewis' usual clarity and ability to penetrate to the uncluttered truth. He also has some very amusing passages in the book, reminiscent of some of the writing in *The Screwtape Letters*. One character, the nicely named Mrs. Fidget, is described thus:

She was always making things too; being in her own estimation (I'm no judge myself) an excellent amateur dressmaker and a great knitter. And of course, unless you were a heartless brute, you had to wear the things. (The Vicar tells me that, since her death, the contributions of that family alone to "sales of work" outweigh all his other parishioners put together.) Mrs. Fidget, as she often said, would "work her fingers to the bone" for her family. They couldn't stop her. Nor could they—being decent people—quite sit still and watch her do it. They had to help. Indeed, they were always having to help—the Vicar says Mrs. Fidget is now at rest. Let us hope she is. What's quite certain is that her family are.

There were also some interesting and illuminating comments, such as "Love, having become a god, becomes a demon", and "To love at all is to be vulnerable. Love anything, and your heart will certainly be wrung and possibly be broken." The book did not do as well as Lewis had hoped, however, nor were his radio talks on the same subject broadcast as widely as he had expected. One of the odd things about Lewis is that he is without doubt a more popular and significant author now than he was while he was alive. Some of his books even did rather badly during his lifetime, and this caused Lewis great distress, particularly after Joy's death and his consequent loneliness.

His life had to a large extent now reverted to what it had been before he met Joy. Many of his friends had gone their separate ways, and he spent term time at Cambridge instead of Oxford, but he still walked, read, and prayed in the same old way—"Say your prayers in the garden early, ignoring steadfastly the dew, the birds and the flowers, and you will come away overwhelmed by its freshness and joy"—and he continued to work as hard as ever. But a certain spark had gone out of his lectures, and his radio broadcasts now lacked the personal touch that had captured so many hearts and minds in the past. Some friends said Lewis was winding down. Perhaps he was.

There are some fascinating portraits of him from these years. His friend George Sayer drove Lewis to Cambridge one day, and they stopped off to walk through a country estate. Lewis was unsure as to whether they should do this, because there was a "Private" sign on the gate to the land. Sayer explained that they were not breaking any law as long as they did no damage. The two men walked along, drinking in the beauty of the English countryside. They soon found themselves in a secluded glade with deer all around. They sat down on a tree trunk, and Lewis was stunned by the loveliness of it all. Small animals danced around as Lewis stared on. "You know, while I was writing the Narnia books I never imagined anything as lovely as this", he said. "Pure white magic."

His health was up and down now, with various internal problems forcing him to his bed. Warnie was still drinking too much and was of limited help to his brother. But the letters were still arriving at The Kilns

Warnie (center) with Mollie and Len Miller, a couple who were devoted to the Lewises. They looked after Warnie after Lewis' death.

and at Cambridge in the hundreds, and Lewis was far too conscientious to ignore them. He engaged a secretary, a young American named Walter Hooper, who after Lewis' death became a priest and an authority on the man he had come to know. Like Joy, Hooper began his relationship with Lewis by writing to him, and then the two men met. Lewis thought so highly of this young man that he began to meet him on a regular, three-times-a-week basis, on Mondays at the Lamb and Flag pub, Thursdays at The Kilns, and Sundays when they attended church together. Lewis made Hooper breakfast, a traditional combination of bacon, eggs, sausages, and toast or buttered scones.

Lewis steadfastly refused to observe his doctor's dietary recommendations. He was not supposed to eat too much fat or protein, but he hardly changed his diet at all after he became ill, enjoying meat, eggs, cheese, and boiled sweets. After a large lunch, he would sleep until four and then revive himself with a cup of tea. From teatime until dinner he wrote and read, had a filling meal, and then relaxed with a book until around ten o'clock, when he went to bed for the night. A typical Lewis day also included lots of tobacco, in a pipe or in cigarettes. It is really no surprise that his health did not improve.

His last book was called *Letters to Malcolm: Chiefly on Prayer*, a series of letters to an imagined acquaintance advising him on the meaning and reality of prayer. "We must lay before Him what is in us, not what ought

Opposite: Lewis in one of his favorite comfortable chairs reading a book in August 1963. It is probably the last photograph ever taken of him. "If only one had time to read a little more: we either get shallow and broad or narrow and deep."

to be in us", he wrote. "If we were perfected, prayer would not be a duty, it would be delight. Some day, please God, it will be." He still wrote essays, and there were other books published after his death, but for the most part, Lewis' writing career was now over. He knew he did not have very long to live and resigned from his position at Cambridge so as to be able to spend the rest of his life at The Kilns.

There were quite regular breakdowns of health now, and before long Lewis was in the Acland Nursing Home for treatment. While he was there, he had a heart attack, fell into a coma, and was given Extreme Unction. But to the amazement of friends as well as doctors and nurses, he was soon sitting up in bed and asking why everybody in the room looked so anxious. He remained in the nursing home for another three weeks, diagnosed as having an infected kidney and blood poisoning. Back at The Kilns a bedroom was made for him downstairs, just as it had been for Joy when she was so ill.

Friends, young and old, came to see Lewis, as if they knew it could be the last opportunity to talk to him. He seemed to be content, they said; indeed, he *was* content. On the evening of November

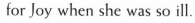

Maureen Moore, daughter of Mrs. Moore, married into the aristocracy and became Lady Dunbar. She remained a loyal friend to Lewis throughout his life.

Lewis' grave in Holy Trinity Church, Headington, Oxford. Pilgrims come from all over the world to visit this place.

21, 1963, he replied to a letter from a child admirer named Philip. "To begin with, may I congratulate you on writing such a remarkably good letter; I certainly could not have written it at your age. And to go on with, thank you for telling me that you like my books, a thing an author is always pleased to hear. It is a funny thing that all the children who have written to me see at once who Aslan is, and grown ups never do! ... Please tell your father and mother how glad I am to hear that they find my serious books of some value." He signed the letter and addressed it, with a smile on his face—letters such as this one gave him great satisfaction. The job done, he went to his bed and to sleep.

He would write no more. He had been feeling unwell and tired for some time, and the next day he felt weak and uneasy. Warnie suggested

Lewis working on his papers at his study desk. He gave, and his books still give, happiness, peace, and love to millions.

that his brother go to bed, and Lewis reluctantly agreed. Warnie took Lewis a cup of tea and found him to be happy enough but drowsy and concerned that his speech was slurred. "At five thirty I heard a crash in his bedroom, and running in, found him lying unconscious at the foot of the bed", wrote Warnie. "He ceased to breathe some three or four minutes after. The following Friday would have been his sixty-fourth birthday."

On the very same day, November 22, President Kennedy was assassinated in Dallas and the author Aldous Huxley died in California. Because of these events, the passing of one of Britain's greatest writers received less attention than it might have, and that would have pleased Plain Jack Lewis, always modest and always the first to make fun of himself. The funeral was small and straightforward, the day was quite cold but sunny and a single candle flickered on Lewis' coffin. Warnie was not there; he was too distraught to leave his bed. Most present were grieving, but grief was really quite unnecessary. Lewis had written and argued for so long that what was to come was far greater than what we have already known. He did not *think* it was so, he did not *believe* it was so, he *knew* it was so. And surely it could be hoped that he was reunited with Joy. "Heaven would have a job to hold me back; and as for Hell, I'd break it into bits." As for Aslan, some say they heard him roar all day, from Oxford to the ends of the Earth.

Chronology

1898   Born on November 29, in Belfast, Ireland.

1905   Family moves to Little Lea.

1908   Mother dies of cancer in August. In September, Lewis is sent to boarding school at Wynyard House in England.

1910   Comes back to Ireland to be schooled at nearby Campbell College.

1911   Returns to England to attend Cherbourg School in Malvern.

1913   Begins studying at Malvern College, "The Coll".

1914   William Kirkpatrick, a family friend, starts tutoring Lewis privately. First World War begins.

1916   Discovers a book (*Phantastes*) by his mentor, George MacDonald. Passes the scholarship exams for Oxford University. Is accepted at University College.

1917   Volunteers for the British Army. Meets Paddy Moore and his mother, Mrs. Janie Moore. Is posted to the front line in France.

1918   Injured in the arm, face, and leg in March. Sent home to recover. Armistice is signed on November 11.

1919   Publishes *Spirits in Bondage* under the pseudonym Clive Hamilton. Moves in with Mrs. Moore and her daughter, Maureen. Continues his studies at Oxford.

1925 Awarded a fellowship in English at Magdalen College, Oxford. Meets J. R. R. Tolkien.

1926 Publishes *Dymer* under the pseudonym Clive Hamilton.

1929 Begins long process of conversion back to Christianity, a turning point in his life. Father dies in September.

1933 Publishes *The Pilgrim's Regress*.

1935 Meets Charles Williams.

1936 Publishes *The Allegory of Love*.

1938 Publishes *Out of the Silent Planet*.

1939 Joins the Inklings. Publishes *Rehabilitations and Other Essays* and *The Personal Heresy*. Second World War begins.

1940 Publishes *The Problem of Pain*.

1941 Begins immensely popular series of radio lectures on the BBC and helps to form the Socratic Club at Oxford.

1942 Publishes *The Screwtape Letters*, *A Preface to Paradise Lost*, and *Broadcast Talks*.

1943 Publishes *Christian Behaviour*, *Perelandra*, and *The Abolition of Man*.

1944 Publishes *Beyond Personality*.

1945 Second World War ends. Charles Williams dies. Lewis publishes *That Hideous Strength* and *The Great Divorce*.

1947 Publishes *Miracles*.

1948 Defeated in a debate at the Socratic Club by Elizabeth Anscombe.

1949 Publishes *Transposition and Other Addresses*.

1950 Receives first letter from Joy Davidman. Publishes *The Lion, the Witch and the Wardrobe*.

1951 Mrs. Moore dies in January. Lewis publishes *Prince Caspian*.

1952 Publishes *Mere Christianity* and *The Voyage of the Dawn Treader*. Joy spends Christmas at The Kilns.

1953 Publishes *The Silver Chair*. Joy and William Gresham divorce, and she moves to England with David and Douglas.

1954 Publishes *The Horse and His Boy* and *English Literature in the Sixteenth Century Excluding Drama*.

1955 Accepts a professorship in medieval and renaissance literature at Magdalene College, Cambridge. Publishes *The Magician's Nephew* and *Surprised by Joy*.

1956 Marries Joy Davidman on April 23 in a civil ceremony at the Oxford Registry Office. Publishes *The Last Battle* and *Till We Have Faces*. Joy is diagnosed with cancer.

1957 Marries Joy in a Christian ceremony at Wingfield Hospital on March 21. Joy's health begins to improve.

1958 Honeymoons in Wales and Ireland with Joy. Publishes *Reflections on the Psalms*.

1959 Joy's cancer returns and spreads rapidly.

1960 Travels to Greece with Joy, who dies on July 13. Publishes *The Four Loves*, *Studies in Words*, and *The World's Last Night and Other Essays*.

1961 Publishes *A Grief Observed* and *An Experiment in Criticism*.

1962 Publishes *They Asked for a Paper: Papers and Addresses*.

1963 On November 22, the same day as President Kennedy is assassinated and Aldous Huxley dies, Lewis passes away at The Kilns.

1964 *Letters to Malcolm: Chiefly on Prayer* is published posthumously.

A Note on Sources

Beginnings

Lewis' early life is thoroughly discussed in two very good biographies, *C. S. Lewis: A Biography* by Roger Lancelyn Green and Walter Hooper (Collins, 1974) and *Jack: C. S. Lewis and His Times* by George Sayer (Harper & Row, 1988). All of these authors actually knew Lewis. Of course, there is nothing quite like the words of Lewis himself, so take a look at *Surprised by Joy* (Geoffrey Bles, 1955), subtitled *The Shape of My Early Life*.

Dreams and Dreaming Spires

Lewis kept a diary between 1922 and 1927 that has been published as *All My Road Before Me* (Collins, 1991) and is essential reading. William Griffin's *Clive Staples Lewis: A Dramatic Life* (Harper & Row, 1986) and A. N. Wilson's *C. S. Lewis: A Biography* (Collins, 1990) also discuss this period in Lewis' life with sympathy and thoroughness.

Friends, Gods, and Devils

Lewis' brother Warnie kept a diary, entitled *Brothers and Friends: The Diaries of Major Warren Hamilton Lewis* (Harper & Row, 1982). He knew Lewis as only a brother could. Humphrey Carpenter wrote about Lewis and his friends in *The Inklings* (Allen & Unwin, 1979).

Narnia

The best place to read about Narnia is, of course, in the Narnia books, all of them published by HarperCollins. Lewis' friend Walter Hooper wrote a book called *Past Watchful Dragons: The Narnian Chronicles of C. S. Lewis* (Fount, 1980), which is a useful guide to the Narnia chronicles.

And Joy Came In

Joy's son Douglas Gresham wrote about his mother and step-father in *Lenten Lands* (Macmillan, 1988). Brian Sibley also wrote about this magnificent relationship in *Shadowlands: The Story of C. S. Lewis and Joy Davidman* (Hodder, 1985), and there is even a film entitled *Shadowlands*, starring Anthony Hopkins as Lewis. The film is not completely accurate, but it is moving and entertaining.

Out of the Shadows

The latter years of Lewis' life are dealt with very well by all of the major biographies. His manner, way of speech, and views are also addressed in James T. Como's *Remembering C. S. Lewis: Recollections of Those Who Knew Him* (Ignatius Press, 2005), first edition entitled *C. S. Lewis at the Breakfast Table and Other Reminiscences* (Collins, 1980). Another book that is good for reference and occasional reading is *The Quotable Lewis* (Tyndale House, 1989), compiled by Wayne Martindale and Jerry Root.

Further Reading

BOOKS BY C. S. LEWIS

Spirits in Bondage (1919)

Dymer (1926)

The Pilgrim's Regress (1933)

The Allegory of Love (1936)

Out of the Silent Planet (1938)

Rehabilitations and Other Essays (1939)

The Personal Heresy (1939)

The Problem of Pain (1940)

The Screwtape Letters (1942)

A Preface to Paradise Lost (1942)

Broadcast Talks (1942)

Christian Behaviour (1943)

Perelandra (1943)

The Abolition of Man (1943)

Beyond Personality (1944)

That Hideous Strength (1945)

The Great Divorce (1945)

Miracles (1947)

Transposition and Other Addresses (1949)

The Lion, the Witch and the Wardrobe (1950)

Prince Caspian (1951)

Mere Christianity (1952)

The Voyage of the Dawn Treader (1952)

The Silver Chair (1953)

The Horse and His Boy (1954)

English Literature in the Sixteenth Century Excluding Drama (1954)

The Magician's Nephew (1955)

Surprised by Joy (1955)

The Last Battle (1956)

Till We Have Faces (1956)

Reflections on the Psalms (1958)

The Four Loves (1960)

Studies in Words (1960)

The World's Last Night and Other Essays (1960)

A Grief Observed (1961)

An Experiment in Criticism (1961)

They Asked for a Paper: Papers and Addresses (1962)

Letters to Malcolm: Chiefly on Prayer (1964)

BOOKS ABOUT C. S. LEWIS

There are books written about Lewis all the time, some of them interesting and helpful, others not so. Below is a list of adult biographies of Lewis that are reliable and useful. There are also commercially available audiocassettes of Lewis reading The Four Loves. *Hearing someone's voice is as important as reading the life of that person.*

Como, James T. (ed.). *Remembering C. S. Lewis: Recollections of Those Who Knew Him*. San Francisco: Ignatius Press, 2005.

Green, Roger Lancelyn, and Walter Hooper. *C. S. Lewis: A Biography*. London: Collins, 1974.

Gresham, Douglas. *Lenten Lands: My Childhood with Joy Davidman and C. S. Lewis*. London: Macmillan, 1988.

Griffin, William. *Clive Staples Lewis: A Dramatic Life*. San Francisco: Harper & Row, 1986.

Hooper, Walter. *Past Watchful Dragons: The Narnian Chronicles of C. S. Lewis*. London: Fount, 1980.

Lewis, Warren Hamilton. *Brothers and Friends: The Diaries of Major Warren Hamilton Lewis*. Eds. Clyde S. Kilby and Marjorie Lamp Mead. San Francisco: Harper & Row, 1982.

Pearce, Joseph. *C. S. Lewis and the Catholic Church*. San Francisco: Ignatius Press, 2003.

Sayer, George. *Jack: C. S. Lewis and His Times*. San Francisco: Harper & Row, 1988.

Sibley, Brian. *Shadowlands: The Story of C. S. Lewis and Joy Davidman*. London: Hodder, 1985.

Wilson, A. N. *C. S. Lewis: A Biography*. London: Collins, 1990.

Picture Sources